The Humanities After the War

THE HUMANITIES
AFTER THE WAR

BY

Wendell L. Willkie

Roscoe Pound

Norman Foerster

Theodore M. Greene

Abraham Flexner

William Macneile Dixon

Gordon Keith Chalmers

EDITED, WITH A PREFACE, BY

Norman Foerster

PRINCETON

PRINCETON UNIVERSITY PRESS

1944

Preface

THE object of this group of essays is to consider the proper place of the humanities in higher education after the war. The war itself placed them in an ambiguous position. On the one hand they were neglected in favor of technical interests essential in the winning of the war. On the other hand what the humanities seek to preserve and promote constituted the very aim of our fighting in a world in danger of being overwhelmed by the inhumanities. Against an expert barbarism misusing science we proposed to defend the values of civilization—justice, decency, tolerance, freedom, including academic freedom to pursue knowledge. These values we had foolishly taken for granted. After the war, if we are not to repeat that tragic error, they must be cherished and extended.

For a hundred years we have allowed the humanities to decline, progressively assigning to them a place decorative or trivial, incidental to the great task of developing science, pure and applied. Science, founded in ancient Greece, at last came into its own, a fact in which every sound humanist rejoices. But with it came the triumph of a philosophy based wholly on science, a naturalistic monism of which the basic dogmas were not and never can be demonstrated by science. It was not science but this naturalistic philosophy that led us to regard science with awe and the humanities with condescension. It was not science but this philosophy that caused us to assume that all knowledge is scientific and that the only method of pursuing knowledge is the method of science. To any such brash one-sidedness the neutral attitude of true science is wholly alien. True science today recoils from it as a dangerous form of armchair philosophy surviving from the nineteenth century and threatening to discredit science itself in the twentieth. If scientists are to repel misguided attacks, they will do so best by drawing sharply the distinction between science and the humanities, by showing that each has its function, methods, and limits, and that they are mutually dependent.

This was suggested, for example, by Dr. Robert A. Millikan when he said, "The scientist provides us with extensive enough information regarding what *is*, but unless we have those among us who tell us also *what makes for*, and what does not make for, our more fundamental well-being, we are lost." At a conference held in London in 1941 on Science and World Order, Professor Einstein in like manner reminded us that science can never give us our aims. "Once these aims exist," he said, "the scientific method furnishes means to realize them. But it cannot furnish the aims themselves. . . . Perfection of means and confusion of aims seem, in my opinion, to characterize our age."

The contrasting but complementary functions of the sciences and the humanities was clearly recognized by Raymond B. Fosdick, the president of the Rockefeller Foundation, in his annual review published in 1942. Suggesting that the peace is feared even more than the war, Dr. Fosdick calls for the common effort of a various leadership. "The economists and political scientists must help us, but so must the physicists and the biologists. And particularly," he ventures to go on, "must we rely on the humanists—the historians, the philosophers, the artists, the poets, the novelists, the dramatists—all those who fashion ideas, concepts, and forms that give meaning and value to life and furnish the patterns of conduct. It is they who really construct the world we live in, and it is they who with sensitive awareness to human perplexity and aspiration and with the power of imaginative presentation can speak effectively to a distracted world." Unhappily there are few signs that our humanists of the imagination are going to be equal to the task; nor is it clear that a distracted world can get along without religion. But certainly Dr. Fosdick is right and salutary in taking seriously, at one and the same time, the sciences (natural and social) and the humanities, in a relationship not of hostility but of cooperation.

With few exceptions the departments of the humanities in higher education are ill prepared for the high task before them. An age of science and of naturalistic philosophy has left its mark upon them. They have misapplied the method of science, and they have adopted views of life that make most of the great writers and thinkers of the world appear of little meaning to the modern age. Lost in a relativism approaching nihilism, they have all but ceased to look for the abiding truths which make the distinction between past and present unimportant. If for a century they have declined in prestige, the reason is partly that they themselves have robbed their great field of its greatness. Today their first task is to refind themselves, not to encourage an intellectual and artistic creativity of any and every sort but rather to lay the critical foundations which will give imaginative presentation a sound direction.

Of the seven essays in this book, five first appeared in 1943 and one in 1942. With these recent essays is included Abraham Flexner's Taylorian Lecture in Oxford, which has new pertinence today. For the privilege of gathering and reprinting this material cordial thanks are due the authors and their publishers: Mr. Willkie (whose article was originally an address at Duke University) and The American Scholar, Spring, 1943; Dr. Pound and The Classical Journal, October, 1943; Professors Greene and Foerster and The Journal of Higher Education, October, 1942, and June, 1943; Dr. Flexner and the Clarendon Press, Oxford, 1928; Professor Dixon and Fortune, April, 1943; President Chalmers (whose article was originally an address at a conference in Denver) and the Social Science Foundation, University of Denver, 1943.

NORMAN FOERSTER

November, 1943

Contents

Freedom and the Liberal Arts

WENDELL L. WILLKIE

I THINK it can be stated as almost an historical truism that the greatest civilizations of history have been the best educated civilizations. And when I speak of education in this sense I do not have in mind what so many today claim as education, namely, special training to do particular jobs. Clearly, in a technological age like ours, a great deal of training is necessary. Some of us must learn how to be mechanics, some how to be architects, or chemists. Some will have a special aptitude for medicine. And a great many will have—or think they have—a mysterious talent inducing them to undertake the practice of law.

But none of these specialties constitutes true education. They are training for skills by which men live. I am thinking, rather, of what we call the liberal arts. I am speaking of education for its own sake: to know for the sheer joy of understanding; to speculate, to analyze, to compare, and to imagine.

Look back across the panorama of history. Is it not true that the pinnacles of civilization have been achieved by the cities and states most proficient in the liberal arts and occupations? In their contributions to the enrichment of human life, the Greeks, I believe, tower above us all. Yet this is not because the Greeks were good navigators, which they were; nor because they were great architects, which indeed they were. It was rather because almost all their leaders—and many of their citizens whose names we do not know—enjoyed knowledge and reverenced the arts. The Greek cities conquered the eastern Mediterranean with the sword. But they conquered posterity with their minds.

The onrush of what we call modern civilization has obscured this essential truth of history. People—some of them in very high places—have openly disparaged the liberal arts. You are told that they are of little help to a man in earning his living or in making a contribution to his fellow men. The thing to do, you are told, is to get trained; learn an occupation; make yourself proficient in some trade or profession. Of course this advice is sound, so far as it goes. But the inference, and sometimes the outright declaration that frequently follows it, strikes at the very roots of our society. The liberal arts, we are told, are luxuries. At best you should fit them into your leisure time. They are mere decorations upon the sterner pattern of life which must be lived in action and by the application of skills. When such arguments gain acceptance that is the end of us as a civilized nation.

Today we are engaged in a desperate war, and we need for the fighting forces almost all the young men who would, normally, have had an opportunity to acquire a liberal education. It is right and proper that these young men should abandon their education temporarily and go forth to fight. It is right and proper that the universities of this country should turn over to the armed forces whatever facilities can be made useful. The government is moving very vigorously in this direction and no patriotic citizen will fail to cooperate.

But I must confess that the attitude in which the conversion of the colleges has been undertaken, together with certain public declarations, fill me with alarm. A few weeks ago, for instance, an Administration spokesman advised all young girls to devote their time to technical training courses in college or to leave college and go to work. Now it is clear that we cannot solve our manpower problem without putting women to work. Yet the fact is that there are millions of women above college age, not needed in their homes or for the care of their children, who are still available. Until these older women are all employed there is no need whatever to drag young women out of the colleges and to deprive them of their one great opportunity for a liberal education. On the contrary, it is a very harmful thing to do. For just now millions of our young men are being deprived of this opportunity, and the per capita percentage of college attendance in the United States is going to fall to a record low for our time. At least, therefore, let us preserve, through the women of America, the continuity of the liberal arts.

In fact, so important are the liberal arts for our future civilization that I feel that education in them should be as much a part of our war planning as the more obviously needed technical training. There will be a certain number of young men in every college who, for one reason or another, are not available for military service. They should be given the facilities whereby they may go on with their education. There will be a certain number who will be returned disabled for active service, but of sound and eager mind. Ways should be provided by which they may continue their education. In addition, there should be some provision in the manpower program for leaving a nucleus in the colleges of men whose aptitudes qualify them as definitely for our long range needs as, let us say, other men are obviously qualified for medicine. So, the structure of the liberal arts colleges will be preserved during the war, and so, minds will be trained and enriched for the humanizing and civilizing of the world to come after.

Furthermore, the men and women who are devoting their lives to such studies should not be made to feel inferior or apologetic in the face of a P.T. boat commander or the driver of a tank. They and all their fellow citizens should know that the preservation of our cultural heritage is not superfluous in a modern civilization; is not a luxury. That it is in fact what gives meaning to that civilization. It is what we are fighting for. And they are serving their country just as surely in fitting themselves to preserve it as are the men who fly the planes or man the ships or fire the guns.

For we cannot win a true victory unless there exists in this country a large body of liberally educated citizens. This is a war for freedom—freedom here and freedom elsewhere. But if we are going to risk our lives for freedom, we must at the same time do all we can to preserve the deep springs from which it flows. Recently we have been prone to think of freedom in purely economic terms. It is true that a man cannot be free unless he has a job and a decent income. But this job and this income are not the sources of his freedom. They only implement it. Freedom is of the mind. Freedom is in the library, around which a university is built. When you range back and forth through the centuries, when you weigh the utterance of some great thinker or absorb the meaning of some great composition, in painting or music or poetry; when you live these things within yourself and measure yourself against them— only then do you become an initiate in the world of the free. It is in the liberal arts that you acquire the ability to make a truly free and individual choice.

Our American higher education for many years has felt the influence of the German university. And it has been a harmful influence. It has encouraged the sacrifice of methods that make for wide intelligence to those which are concerned only with highly specialized knowledge; it has held that the subject is more important than the student; that knowledge is more important than understanding; that science, in itself, can satisfy the soul of man; and that intelligent men should not be allowed to concern themselves with politics and the administration of state. Such matters should be left to trained politicians. President Hopkins of Dartmouth has stated these trends more clearly than anyone I know and has pointed out that "it would be a tragic paradox if, as a result of the war, we were to allow our system of higher education to be transformed into the type of education which has made it so easy for a crowd of governmental gangsters like Hitler's outfit to commandeer a whole population."

[4]

The destruction of the tradition of the liberal arts, at this crisis in our history, when freedom is more than ever at stake, would mean just that. It would be a crime, comparable, in my opinion, with the burning of the books by the Nazis. And it would have approximately the same results. Burn your books —or, what amounts to the same thing, neglect your books—and you will lose freedom, as surely as if you were to invite Hitler and his henchmen to rule over you.

The preservation of our system of liberal education during the war will make an enormous difference in the moral and human tone of our society in the future, of the very atmosphere in which the peace is made, and, since we are not an isolated society, of all civilization after the war. Let me remind you of Irwin Edman's recent fine statement of the significance of the very word "humanities." "It is not trivial art or playful thought. It is the name for the whole of the tradition of civilized life which from the Greeks down has accented freedom in political life and individuality and creativeness in personal relations, creativeness in art, and originality in the experiment of living which is each individual's opportunity. If the humanities, or the humanistic temper which they promote, are permitted to lapse now, we shall have lost the peace before we have gained it, and the real victory after the war will be to the way of life, inhuman, tyrannical, mechanical, of those whom we shall outwardly have conquered."

In pleading for the humanities I am not preaching any gospel of high-browism. The relationship between a liberal education and freedom is good sound American doctrine. There are hundreds of colleges in this land of more or less advanced education, and in recent years they have been graduating thousands of students every year. Naturally, all of these graduates are not proficient in the liberal arts. And yet no matter how they may have neglected their college courses, or how overzealously they may have specialized, they have won some measure of equality with all the great minds and all the challenging personalities of all time. That fact has been immeasurably important in making our American doctrine of equality a real and living doctrine.

I regret that during the last several decades we have had a tendency to overlook this important American fact. And I think we are paying the penalty for our shortsightedness in unexpected ways.

For instance, there has been a trend recently toward what is called "leadership"—but what is really nothing more than the idolization of individual men. In Italy, Mussolini took the title of Il Duce—the Leader—on the grounds that he was the one man who could fulfill the destiny of the Italian people. Not long after, in Germany, Hitler began calling himself Der Führer. The politics advocated by these men were totalitarian, and therefore, antipathetic to our way of life. Yet the overemphasis on single individuals has gone on, even in countries which are fighting totalitarianism now. Everywhere you turn today, you find people clinging to certain men who have been exalted in the public mind out of all proportion to their talents, however great. In Russia there is Joseph Stalin, in China, Generalissimo Chiang Kai-shek, in Britain, Winston Churchill, in the United States, Franklin Roosevelt. The stature of these men is in every case out of the ordinary and they deserve the high positions they have won. And yet, dare we say that any one of them is indispensable? The moment we say that, our world must change.

I do not know all the reasons for this emphasis on single individuals. But I do perceive a connection, here in America at any rate, between that emphasis and the neglect of the liberal arts. Had we more faith in liberal education, we would have, I believe, more faith in ourselves—more faith in the great leavening process of democracy, which forever pushes new men to the top.

I have had the privilege of meeting most of the great men of our time and of conversing with them intimately. I have talked with and know all the allied leaders I have just mentioned, and many more besides. Yet I can say truthfully that, however impressive their abilities—and I have found them impressive—I saw nothing in them that could not conceivably be duplicated in Akron, Ohio, where I practiced law for many years, or here at Duke University. I think it was William Howard Taft who said that you could find a man fit to sit on the Supreme Court Bench of the United States, in any town in America of more than 5,000 population. Possibly Mr. Taft exaggerated. Yet surely the *principle* has been proved time after time in American history. The vast American educational system has set men free—free not alone to serve, but free also to lead. Education is the mother of leadership.

Now I think there is another phenomenon of our time which is linked with our failure to grasp the real significance of liberal education. This is an excessive indulgence in the practice of what is known as censorship and propaganda. Of course, censorship of military matters is necessary in order to conduct a war. But this principle is being daily, if not hourly, abused and extended to many other matters that have no military significance whatsoever. More and more the doctrine of telling us what we should know is being adopted.

It is of course natural for men who attain high office to seek to preserve themselves from the ordeal of public criticism and to attempt to stimulate approval of their policies and so to perpetuate themselves in power.

And those who are suppressing free discussion among us and our allies have of course a rationalization for their policy. They say that they must conduct political warfare. In the conduct of political warfare, they claim, it is damaging to say certain things. The enemy, they tell us, picks them up, distorts them, uses them against us. All this, of course, is true enough. But what of it? The time has never been when men did not seek to distort the utterances of their enemies for their own advantage. And what has won out in the long battle? Always the truth. Spread the facts, analyze them, debate them, make them available to all the world. *There is no other form of political warfare that can possibly win the great political struggle in which we are engaged. Truth alone can win it.*

Is not this worship of leaders, this willingness to be told what to think, this unquestioning acceptance of unnecessary restrictions on our freedom of speech, is not all this part of the same trend—the trend away from self-reliant judgment, the trend away from the little towns, the trend away from the dignity of the common man, the trend away from liberal education, by which men achieve equality in fact as well as in law? We have seen these impulses take root in other countries, which are now our enemies. We have seen them carried to their dreadful conclusions. We have seen the exaltation of government, the abasement of culture, and the resulting violation of all that civilization cherishes. We have seen the devolution of human aspiration. It is a tragedy as great as men have ever witnessed. And it is our task, a task in which we shall be engaged for the rest of our lives, first to stop it, and then to repair it.

There is much discussion now—and quite properly—of the matter of war aims. Yet I have listened to some of these speeches with misgiving. I have shuddered to hear a member of our government planning, when the war is over, to police the education of our late enemies, after the traditional manner of conquerors. To disarm those enemies, yes. To take whatever measures are necessary to prevent rearming, yes. To remove from the necks of the people an enslaving totalitarian rule, certainly. But having done that, education is another matter. It must grow out of and carry on a native culture. To determine the nature and manner of their own education is the right of men everywhere. And alien ideals superimposed by force will only produce resentment and hatred.

Too many of the planners, I feel, are trying to look ahead by looking backward. Too many are seeking the future in the past. I find in many of their speeches an attempt to solve everything by their pet economic theories—the same attempt that has nearly ruined us during the last ten or fifteen years. The study and practice of sound economics is indispensable to a successful solution of the peace. And yet even sound economics cannot define the aim of the peace, nor the aim of the war. To discover that aim we must go deeper. We must establish beyond any doubt the equality of men. And we shall find this equality, not in the different talents which we severally possess, nor in the different incomes which we severally earn, *but in the great franchise of the mind*, the universal franchise, which is bounded neither by color, nor by creed, nor by social status. Open the books, if you wish to be free.

The Humanities in an Absolutist World

ROSCOE POUND

Man's significant achievement is civilization, the continual raising of human powers to a higher unfolding, a continually increasing mastery of, or control over, external or physical nature and over internal or human nature. Civilization is an accumulative activity. Both its aspects, control of physical nature and control of human nature, are added to from generation to generation and the whole is an accumulation of ages. In the present, the progress of control over physical nature, of harnessing external nature to man's use, has been so rapid and has been carried so far beyond what had been taken to be the limit of human powers, that it has all but blinded us to the other side, the control of internal nature. But in truth the two are interdependent. It is the control over internal or human nature which has made possible the division of labor by which the harnessing of physical nature has been made possible. If men were subject to constant aggression from their fellows, if they could not safely assume that they could go about their daily tasks free from attack, there could not be the experiment and research and investigation which have enabled man to inherit the earth and to maintain and increase that inheritance. The accumulation from generation to generation would be dissipated if it were not for the check upon man's destructive instincts which is achieved through accumulated control of internal nature. But the control over external nature relieves the pressure of the environment in which man lives and enables the accumulated control over internal nature to persist and increase.

In the history of civilization the outstanding period, from the standpoint of control over internal nature, is classical antiquity, the Greek-Hellenistic-Roman civilization, which happily kept no small degree of continuity during the Middle Ages, and was revived at the Renaissance. This period is as marked for one side of civilization as the nineteenth century and the present are likely to be held in the future for the other side. Indeed, the civilization of ancient Greece, carried on in the Hellenistic era and established for the world by the organizing and administrative genius of the Romans, is a decisive element in the civilization of today.

Art, letters, oratory, philosophy, history writing, are an inheritance from the Greeks. Law, administration, politics, are an inheritance from the Romans. The Greeks even worked out the field tactics to which the military science of today has reverted. Greek and Latin are a preponderant element in the languages which derive from Western Europe. Thus they enter decisively into our thinking, writing, and speaking, and thus into our doing. The last of the Caesars fell a generation ago. But the principles of adjusting human relations and ordering human conduct worked out in theory by Greek philosophers and made into law by Roman jurists of the days of the first Caesars govern in the tribunals of today. Latin was the universal language from the establishment of Roman hegemony and of Roman law as the law of the world for at least nineteen hundred years. All modern literature in all languages is full of allusions to the classics; of allusions to persons and events and stories out of the poets and dramatists and historians of Greece and Rome. One who knows nothing of the great authors of antiquity is cut off from the great authors of the modern world as well. To take but one example, a generation which grows up without anyone knowing Horace has missed something irreplaceable. To cease to teach the classics is to deprive the oncoming generation of opportunity of fruitful contact with a decisive element in the civilization in which it is to live. A generation cut off from its inherited past is no master of its present. What men do is conditioned by the materials with which they must work in doing it. On one side of our civilization these are for the most significant part materials bequeathed to us by the Greeks and the Romans.

But we are told that we are entering upon a new era. The past is to be canceled. We are to begin with a clean slate. Our accumulated control over external nature has gone so far that there remains only the task of making it available for universal human contentment. Then there will be no occasion for control over internal nature. The causes of envy and strife are to go with want and fear. Mankind will settle down to a passive enjoyment of the material goods of existence and will neither require nor desire anything more.

There are abundant signs of a significant change from the ideas and ideals and values which governed in the immediate past. It is not, however, a change to something wholly new. It is largely a reversion to something with which the student of classical antiquity is well acquainted; to modes of thought against which Socrates argued with the Sophists, about which Plato and Aristotle wrote in founding a science of politics, about which Stoics debated with Epicureans, which Christianity put down, for a time at least, when it closed the skeptical and Epicurean schools of philosophy.

Whatever the confident self-styled advanced thinkers of today may be looking forward to, the immediate actual result is a cult of force. We seem to be listening again to Thrasymachus, who argued that the shepherd protects the sheep in order to shear them for wool and slaughter them for mutton, and in the same way the political ruler protects the governed in order to be able to despoil them. The Sophists are coming into their own in ethics, and Machiavelli is hailed as a prophet in a realism which in law and in politics takes force to be the reality and those who wield the force of politically organized society, as the representatives of force, to be the actualities of the legal order and of the political order. A favorite phrase of the realist is "the brute facts"; a phrase used not in sadness that there should be such facts, but with a certain relish, as if brutality were the test of reality and the discovery of brute facts argued superior intelligence and discernment. In practice this makes force a test of significance. The significant things in the world are force and the satisfaction of material wants. Education must be shaped to the exigencies of these. Nothing else is to be taught or learned. Such a doctrine carried into practice, a regime to that pattern, would indeed give us a new world. But it would be new by reverting to a very old type.

Biologists tell us that what they call giantism in an organism is a sign of decadence. When the organism has developed to giant proportions, the next step is decline and the ultimate step is fall. In the same way, there are times in the history of civilization when things seem to have become too big for men to manage them. They get out of hand. The social order ceases to function efficiently. There is a gradual breakdown, followed after a time of chaos and anarchy by a gradual rebuilding of a social order, which in turn may develop a bigness beyond human powers of management and so break down. It may be significant that today the air is full of grandiose schemes for world organization.

The Hellenistic world was in such an era. The greater and richer part of the civilized world had been swallowed up in the empire of Alexander. An age of independent city-states was succeeded by one of great military empires ruled autocratically. Later, the Roman hegemony, in which, as it culminated in the Empire, every free man in the civilized world was a Roman citizen, the law of the city of Rome had become the law of the world, and all political authority was centralized in the first citizen of Rome, was another era of the same kind. It is significant that the first citizen of such a state became a military autocrat. The mark of thinking of such times is likely to be disillusionment. Epicureanism arose in the period of the successors of Alexander, and grew increasingly strong in the Hellenistic era. It throve in the corresponding period of Roman history, the Empire from Augustus to Diocletian and Constantine. It was the most firmly intrenched of the Greek schools of philosophy, although it has contributed the least to the general progress of thought. It was so well fitted to a period of bigness and incipient decay that the Epicureans were the last school to give way before the rise of Christianity. When the schools of philosophy were abolished, they were the most widespread and tenacious of the anti-Christian sects.

Today, in another era of unmanageable bigness, we come upon tenacious give-it-up philosophies once more. Epicurus was wholly indifferent to the form of political organization of society. The real point in existence was to lead a happy life. If he lived under a wise ruler, the man seeking a happy life need have no fear of being disturbed. He could pursue a serene, untroubled existence. If the ruler was a tyrant, the wise man, like Br'er Rabbit, would "jes' lie low" and so escape the tyrant's notice and live an undisturbed life of happiness. Today what Epicurus put as happiness, current social philosophies put as security. The ideal is an undisturbed enjoyment of the means of satisfying material wants. Put concretely it seems to be a vested right in a life job with an assured maximum wage, fixed short hours, allowing much time for leisure at stated periods, a prohibiting of anyone from an overactivity which might give him an advantage, and compelling all to a regimented minimum exertion that would obviate the exciting of envy, and a guaranteed pension at the age of sixty, dispensing with the need of providing one's own reserve. This is the ideal existence Epicurus pictured—the condition of a happy life, the condition of perfect mental equilibrium, neither perturbed nor perturbable. In contrast, the last century identified security with liberty. Men sought security from interference with their activities. They sought to be secure against aggression so that they might freely do their part in the division of labor in a competitive economic order. They sought to be secure against governmental action except so far as was necessary to free them from aggressions of others. Now, instead of seeking to be secure against government, men expect to be made secure by government. But they expect to be secure in a new way; not to be secure in their activities, but to be secure against necessity of activity, to be secure in satisfaction of their material wants with a minimum of required individual activity.

Very likely the change reflects the exigencies of a bigger and more crowded world. Possibly it is due in part to the development of luxury, leading to disinclination to the free competitive carving out of a place for oneself which the last century took for happiness. At any rate, freedom from worry about what one can achieve, renouncing of ambition to do things, and acceptance of political events as they may happen, go together as an accepted philosophy of wise living, as they did in the social philosophy of Epicurus.

Marxian economic realism has much in common with the Epicurean social philosophy. The static ideal of a happy life is to be attained as we get rid of classes. It is assumed that when property is abolished all competition between human beings will cease. Everyone will live undisturbed, without ambition, without envy, and so freed from strife. Once the class struggle has been brought to an end, Marx looked forward to the same social ethical result as Epicurus. But there is nothing in the history of civilization or in experience of human relations in a crowded world to warrant such assumptions. We may be sure that after property is abolished men will still want and claim to use things which cannot be used by more than one or by more than one at a time. It is not likely that there will always be enough at all times of every material good of existence to enable everyone at every moment to have or do all that he can wish, so that no contentions can arise as to possession or use and enjoyment. Nor is it likely in any time which we can foresee that there will be no conflicts or overlappings of the desires and demands involved in the individual life. Such ideas, however, seem to go with bigness such as the economic unification of the world has brought about in the present century.

Along with the disillusioned or give-it-up philosophies of such a time there goes a changed attitude toward government. Instead of wanting to do things, men want to have things done for them, and they turn to government to do for them what they require for a happy life. But they have no wish to be active in government. They turn to absolute political ideas. Eras of bigness and autocracy have gone together. Today while we all do lip service to democracy there is a manifest turning to autocracy. The democracy is to be an absolute democracy. Those who wield its authority are not to be hampered by constitutions or laws or law. What they do is to be law because they do it. They are to be free to make us all happy by an absolute power to pass on the goods of existence to us by such measure of values as suits them.

Such ideas of a happy life, and of politically organized society as the means of assuring that happy life, require an omnicompetent government. They require a government with absolute power to carry out the plan of an undisturbed life of serenity, free from all envy, want, or worry, by control of all activity no less than of all material goods. The restless must be held down, the active must be taught to keep quiet in a passive happiness, those inclined to question the economic order must be taught to accept the regime of security in which their material wants are satisfied. Hence such a polity must of necessity take over education. Men are to be educated to fit into the regime of government-provided material happiness. Those things which will tend to achieve and maintain such a regime are to be taught. All else is to be given up. Either it will hinder the bringing about and making permanent of the new regime or it will tend to impair it when established. There is no place for any of it in the ideal regime.

Applied to international relations, the give-it-up philosophies must be wonderfully heartening doctrine for dictators. Applied to internal administration they are proving wonderfully heartening doctrine for bureaucrats. Can we doubt that a sense of helplessness in the Hellenistic era and again in the era of the later Roman Empire led to general acceptance of a philosophy that taught to let the government run itself or the governors run it in their own way? Can we doubt that a sense of helplessness in our time, a feeling of helplessness to make international relations conform to ideals, leads to acquiescence in theories of force; or that difficulty in an overcrowded world to make adjustments of private relations according to law achieve ideal results, leads to a theory of a law as simply a threat of state force and hence of law as whatever officials do in applying that force?

But if we are moved at times to feel helpless and give up to power and force, those who wield the force of politically organized society have no misgivings. They have supreme confidence that the omnicompetence of the state means the omnicompetence of the officials who act in the name and by the authority of the state, and are ready, assuming themselves to be ex-officio experts, to prescribe detailed regulations for every human activity.

We recognize such conditions when we look at them as they are manifest in the older parts of the world. We have not been prepared to see them as they have been developing gradually but steadily in our own polity. As a leader in American legal education has put it, it is simply a question of what we expect government to do. If we expect it to provide for all our wants by a benevolent paternal care and maternal solicitude, we must expect to surrender to it all responsibility and invest it—and that means those persons who carry it on—with all power. Such a regime is fostered by the exigencies of war. But it was growing long before the war and independent of war conditions. The give-it-up philosophies were taught and preached before and apart from the war. They have been urged by a strong group in both English and American institutions of learning and are propagated today by teachers who advocate an unrestrained administrative power over liberty and property.

What is happening, what is to happen, to the humanities in such a time?

In this connection we must note another characteristic of the time, namely, distrust of reason. In this respect also the thought of today is akin to that of Epicurus. We are taught by the psychological realists that consciously or unconsciously men do what they wish to do and then justify what they have done by reasons conjured up by a desire to be reasonable, which nevertheless are not the real determinants of their behavior. Consequently, by not distinguishing reason from reasons, reason comes to be regarded as a mere name for specious justifying to oneself of what one desires to do and does accordingly. Reason is taken to be illusion. The reality is taken to be the wish, achieved by force or by the force of a politically organized society. This is brought out notably in the difference between the biographies of the last century and those of today. The biographies of the last century were taken up with what their subject did and how he did it. They assume that he had reasons for what he did which were consistent with his purposes and professions, and that his mistakes were due to miscalculation, unless the evidence constrains a different conclusion. The biographies of today are taken up with their subject's hidden motives; if not very creditable, so much the better as the biographer sees it. The evidence does not disclose the motives. The assumed motives interpret the evidence. If the biographer can show that George Washington's motives may be made out to have been not always very creditable, it only goes to show that his actions were after all merely phenomena and to remind us that it is unscientific to apply our subjective ideas of praise and blame to phenomena.

At any rate, we can find one powerful antidote to such teachings in the humanities, and it is perhaps for that reason that the advocates of so-called realism would suppress the teaching of them. At the beginning of the present century the German Emperor objected to the education which, he said, trained the youth to be young Greeks and Romans instead of to be modern Germans. But the results of education to be Germans ought to give us pause if we think to make Americans by an education that seeks to make Americans to a pattern of a land given up to satisfaction of material wants provided by a regime of absolute government.

But I hear people say the aggregate of knowledge has become so vast that teaching must be confined to those things that count in the world of today. There are translations of the classics available in English and those whose interests lead them to explore the writings of antiquity can find what they seek in those translations. It is a waste of the time that must be given to the things of today to study difficult dead languages in order to find what translations have made accessible in modern languages. The time is needed for the natural and physical sciences, which teach us how to harness more of external nature to producing the material goods of human existence, and to the social sciences, which are to teach us how those goods are to be made to satisfy human desires. Here we have three fallacious propositions: (1) that education is only the acquisition of knowledge, (2) that even the best translation is or can be a substitute for the original of a classic, and (3) that the social sciences are so far advanced that we may rely upon them for objective judgments of the social order and of the problems and phenomena of ethics and economics and politics and jurisprudence. We have to learn the formulas of the social scientists as we once learned the formulated dogmas of the natural and physical sciences. Let us look at these propositions.

Knowledge as such is worth little without knowing how to use it. It is likely to be so up-to-date that it is out of date tomorrow. Discrimination, reasoned judgment, and creative thinking must work upon knowledge to make it fruitful. No one can approach a mastery of all the details of knowledge in even the narrowest field. But he can attain the wisdom that will enable him to lay hold upon those details when and where he requires them and to make something of them. Without this, the study of up-to-date subjects as merely so many tracts of knowledge is futile. Very likely the supposed facts will have ceased to be so regarded by scientists as soon as they have been learned. The wise scholar, however, knows how to find them as they stand at the moment and appraise them for his purposes, and he can often do this although he approaches a subject in which he never had a formal course.

Wisdom is not gained by the use of translations. It is not acquired when students write confidently about Aristotle without having read or being able to read a line of him. It is not developed by slovenly use of language such as follows from never having been compelled to compare the same thought expressed in two languages and brought to see how different it may appear unless the translator is sure of the words no less than of the idea. What teacher of today has not seen confused thought bred of loose writing, due to lack of the disciplined use of words which is acquired by learning the languages from which even our scientific terminology is derived? What teacher has not encountered the type of student who wants to write a thesis on poetic usage and expects to use Pope's *Iliad* to show him the usage of Homer? Who has not met students of church history who cannot read the New Testament in the original, students writing on medieval philosophy and essaying to criticize a great thinker who cannot read a word of Thomas Aquinas in the tongue in which he wrote, students of legal history who cannot read *Magna Carta* as it was written, students of history who must take the significant historical documents at second or third hand? I have too often witnessed the pathetic struggles of would-be students of our legal history to handle the monuments of our law in the Middle Ages with no adequate grasp of the language in which they were written. I shall not soon forget the graduate student who thought he could read the Code of Justinian by the light of nature and was astonished to find that *conventus* did not, as he supposed, mean "convent" but meant "agreement." Nor are such things confined to students. Who of us has not had occasion to feel for the earnest teacher who missed the fundamentals of his education in school and college and now is found struggling to gain what too late he perceives he sorely needs? A great injustice had been done to all of these by leading them to think they were acquiring an adequate foundation for what they desired to do, and leaving them to discover their mistake too late.

We are told that those things which are not indispensable must in education in a democracy give way to those which are indispensable. As to this one must make three observations. In the first place, it assumes that democracy requires a common training for all, a training in the mechanic arts and the sciences behind them, and in social sciences on the model of the physical sciences. No one is to be allowed an opportunity of development outside of this program of preparation for material production and politics. Secondly, it assumes that education is complete on leaving school, and hence that there need be no preparation for scholarly self-development of an element needed in any other than a stagnant or enslaved population. Third, it assumes that the social sciences are or can be such as the physical and natural sciences are; that ultimate truths as to economics and politics and sociology are impartable by teaching, and that knowledge of these truths is essential to a democratically organized people.

I have no quarrel with the social sciences. I am now in my forty-fourth year of teaching jurisprudence, and for forty of those years have taught it from the sociological standpoint. I have urged the importance of ethics and economics and politics and sociology in connection with law in forty years of law-school teaching. But I do not deceive myself as to those so-called sciences. So far as they are not descriptive, they are in continual flux. In the nature of things they cannot be sciences in the sense of physics or chemistry or astronomy. They have been organized as philosophies, have been worked out on the lines of geometry, have been remade to theories of history, have had their period of positivism, have turned to social psychology, and are now in an era of neo-Kantian methodology in some hands and of economic determinism or psychological realism or relativist skepticism or phenomenological intuitionism in other hands. They do not impart wisdom; they need to be approached with acquired wisdom. Nothing of what was taught as economics, political science, or sociology when I was an undergraduate is held or taught today. Since I left college, sociology has gone through four, or perhaps even five, phases. Indeed, those who have gone furthest in these sciences in the immediate past were not originally trained in them. They are not foundation subjects. They belong in the superstructure.

Notice how extremes meet in a time of reaction to absolutist political ideas. In an autocracy men are to be trained in the physical and natural sciences so as to promote material production. They are to be trained in the social sciences so as to promote passive obedience. In an absolutist democracy men are to be trained in the physical and natural sciences because those sciences have to do with the means of satisfying material wants. They are to be trained in the social sciences because those sciences have to do with politically organized society as an organization of force whereby satisfaction of material wants is to be attained. As an important personage in our government has told us, the rising generation must be taught what government can do for them. The relegation of the humanities to a back shelf, proposed by the Kaiser at the beginning of the present century, has been taken over to be urged as a program of a democracy. Such ideas go along with the rise of absolute theories of government throughout the world. An omnicompetent government is to tell us what we shall be suffered to teach, and the oncoming generation is to be suffered to learn nothing that does not belong to a regime of satisfying material wants by the force of a political organization of society. It is assumed that there is nothing in life but the satisfaction of material wants and force as a means of securing satisfaction of them.

America was colonized in a similar period of absolutist political ideas—in the era of the Tudor and Stuart monarchy in England, of the old regime of which the rule of Louis XIV was the type in France, of the monarchy set up by Charles V in Spain, of the establishment of the absolute rule of the Hapsburgs in Austria. England of the Puritan Revolution shook these ideas violently and at the Revolution of 1688 definitely cast them off for two centuries. The colonists who came to America settled in the wilderness in order to escape them. When we settled our own polity at the end of the eighteenth century, we established it as a constitutional democracy, carefully guarded against the reposing of unlimited power anywhere. Moreover, these early Americans, because they did not believe in an omnicompetent government or superman rulers, set up institutions for liberal education. Within six years after their arrival in the wilderness in the new world, the founders of Massachusetts set up a college in order that there might continue to be a learned ministry after their ministers who had come from the English universities were laid in the dust. As our country expanded in its westward extension across the continent, state after state in its organic law provided for a state university in order that liberal learning might be the opportunity of everyone. It was not till our era of expansion was over and one of industrialization began that state institutions for mechanical education were more and more established. But these for a generation did not greatly disturb the humanities. The movement to displace them is a phenomenon of the era of bigness.

Outward forms of government are no panacea. We can't do better than we try to do. If we are content to lapse into a revived Epicureanism, if we are content to seek nothing more than a general condition of undisturbed passivity under the benevolent care of an omnicompetent government, we can very well leave education to the sciences which have to do with providing the material goods of existence and those which teach us how the government secures or is to secure them for us. If we are not content with being, as Horace put it, pigs of the drove of Epicurus, but seek to live active, human lives, even at some risk of envy and strife and wish for things unattainable, we must stand firm against projects which will cut our people off from the great heritage of the past and deny them the opportunity of contact with the best that men have thought and written in the history of civilization.

I cannot think that, when what is meant by the displacement of the humanities is brought home to them, the intelligent people of America will consent to bow the knee to Baal. I am confident that, as Milton put it, we shall be able to speak words of persuasion to abundance of reasonable men, once we make plain the plausible fallacy behind the idea of teaching only the indispensables, and that the physical and the social sciences are the indispensables. We can have a democracy without having a people devoted solely to production and consumption. Those who are fighting to preserve the humanities are working for a democracy that can endure. One which sinks into materialistic apathy must in the end go the way of the peoples which have succumbed to the perils of mere bigness in the past.

A University Prepared for Victory

NORMAN FOERSTER

IN America the university is today dedicating its physical plant, its expert knowledge, and its moral energies to the winning of the war. It is united in a common effort with the armed forces, the munition factories, and the basic industries. It is wholeheartedly performing a difficult task for which it was ill prepared. Like the schools from which its students came, it had failed to develop before hostilities the widespread knowledge of languages, mathematics, physics, geography, and other subjects fundamental in the conduct of a global war.

Is the university to be caught equally unprepared for peace?

When our young men—and young women—return from the wars, many of them will return to the university. What kind of university will it be then? Will it be the university they remember, unchanged by the most violent storm in human history? Will it be a meaningless prolongation of the wartime university, a university focusing its forces upon the destruction of human beings?

A similar problem confronted the American university of 1918, and the university failed to solve it, scarcely made an effort to solve it. It merely drifted. It was no better than the society which it gaily served, an acquisitive society materialistic in its interests, unhealthy in its pleasures, disillusioned in its ideals, a society moving blindly toward the disaster which came in 1929 and matured in 1939. Admittedly, the pressure of this society was enormous, not only in America but also in the associated powers, England and France; even the pathological fool who precipitated the conflict described with tolerable accuracy the decadence of the great democratic societies in the nineteen-twenties. We know the result: the collapse of France, the recovery of England only because of the breathing spell made possible by the Channel, and the slow opening of eyes in the aloof democracy on our side of the Atlantic. In dire strain and agony the two great English-speaking democracies summoned up forgotten spiritual reserves in a supreme effort made necessary only because they had been so blind and flaccid. For this tragedy the university after 1918 must accept its share of responsibility, a university aimlessly expansive, materialistic in its interpretation of life, neutral, skeptical or cynical in respect to ideal values, asserting only the pacifism of those who do not want to be disturbed, professing only the humanitarianism of those who have forgotten the true worth of man.

Is the university, and the society in which it functions, determined to profit by its mistakes after the last war? Unquestionably it is—in the economic and political realms. Everywhere within and without the universities the spokesmen of our society are urging plans for the economic and political reorganization of the world. Much the same thing happened during the last war, though the reforms proposed were less drastic and therefore, it would seem, easier of attainment. Why were the results so dismal? The answer would appear to be: because no economic and political reorganization can succeed unless it is accompanied and sustained by a moral and intellectual reorientation. External rearrangements must finally depend upon a change in men's minds and wills. Systems may be good or bad; but even bad systems work fairly well when the men living with them are good, and the best systems work badly when the men are bad. As Guizot put it in his history of civilization, "All the great developments of the internal man have turned to the profit of society, all the great developments of the social state to the profit of individual man." Of the truth of the latter statement we are today well convinced; of the truth of the former we are far from adequately aware. In our zeal for the external we have all but forgotten the internal.

Not wholly forgotten it. We say that the present war is not a war of rival powers; we say that it is not even a war of rival systems, fascist versus democratic; we say that it is a war of the values underlying the systems, that we are fighting for a world in which we shall have sound, civilized values and not the distorted, primitive values which the Axis powers are trying to impose. So much we see and profess. But our conception of values is, in the main, negative, freedom from one thing or another; freedom from religious persecution, freedom from muzzled mouths and press, freedom from physical want, freedom from fear of our neighbors. Our four freedoms are essentially negative. Even so, they are probably potent enough to sustain us in the war. Once the war is won, however, once the unsocial impulses that are checked in war are released and rebound, we shall have to be ready to develop some positive and constructive values, or we shall once again return to the fleshpots.

Considered positively, the four freedoms may be summed up in one word: opportunity. Clearly, opportunity is good, but how good it is depends on how it is used, what ends are sought for, once people are free to seek ends. As Mr. Roosevelt remarked during the campaign, freedom of speech is not worth much unless you have something to say. He might have added that freedom of religion is not worth much unless you have a religion or are seeking one. If we are to affirm positive values as a dynamic force in our society, we shall have to ask, Freedom for what? Opportunity for what?

Again some sort of answer is ready: we propose to reaffirm and make real the dignity of man, the significance and worth of the single person. But again the answer is desperately vague. Anyone who goes about among his fellows today, like an inquisitive Socrates, asking people what they mean by "the dignity of man," will get replies vaguer than at any time since the gadfly of Athens plagued his fellow citizens. The only definite reply is likely to be that human dignity consists in having "the necessaries of life," that is, "the well-being of animals," since this view makes no distinction between man and other forms of life. It is a view that seems to satisfy most of those who place political and economic planning in the foreground. In their paradoxical logic, the internal excellence of man is found in externals, in things, in a certain minimum of possessions, from which they go on to argue that lasting peace depends upon a constantly rising standard of living throughout the world. They forget that, whatever importance we must assign to the means of living, the means are not the ends, and that it is the ends that determine human dignity.

If we are to escape from this confusion and from the terrible frustrations and disappointments to which it will lead in practical affairs, we shall have to achieve in the coming years an intellectual and spiritual reorientation, and we shall have to achieve it in three phases. First, in the realm of abstract thought we need a sufficiently clear conception of the true worth of man. Second, in the realm of emotion we need a concrete, moving image of man as he ought to be, a compelling picture of human excellence. Third, in the realm of action we need the will to realize this image for oneself and the will to help others to realize it for themselves.

To perform this supremely difficult task is the responsibility, the high and inescapable responsibility, of the humanities: of the interpretation of human life by history, by literature and the arts, by philosophy, by religion.

Aside from its inherent difficulty, the task is made trebly formidable by the indifference and frivolity of the public in its attitude toward these fields of activity and by the want of conviction and vision prevailing among those who are active in these fields. The public lives in the present, not in history; looks to literature and the arts for entertainment and the adornment of life; leaves philosophy to the harmless specialist; and has been all but weaned away from its religious loyalties. Meanwhile, the historian has preferred facts to interpretation, or has adopted some kind of economic interpretation of the past; literary and other artists, together with academic professors of literature and the arts, have been largely content with problems of technique or the amassing of closely observed facts; philosophers have reflected the material interests of the age and placed man more and more in the flux of nature; and religious leaders, in most denominations, have grown more and more secular.

In the face of this situation among laymen and specialists, it may seem all but hopeless to bring about an intellectual and spiritual reorientation. Yet even a glance into the past is enough to remind us that from age to age great changes in the intellectual and spiritual climate do occur, and a glance at the present world, with its expectancy of revolutionary change, is enough to suggest that a fundamental change is now due. There is much to support the view expressed by Theodore M. Greene (see the following chapter, "The Realities of Our Common Life") that the present conflict is a surface manifestation of a deeper crisis. "We all know," says Mr. Greene, "that the military conflict reflects underlying political and economic difficulties which must be solved if peace, when it comes, is to endure. Underlying these economic, social, and political difficulties, in turn, there is the stratum of cultural values and modes of thought; our crisis is in a very real sense a cultural crisis. Finally, underlying this cultural level is the still more profound level of spiritual commitment and religious faith." The malady of the age, in short, goes deep, and will not be remedied by the superficial treatment of symptoms.

If in this crisis of civilization the university is to serve the state and nation fundamentally, its departments of the humanities will have to set their house in order. Unhappily, the great majority of teachers in these departments are scarcely aware that the main crisis is inside their own fields. They view with alarm the fact that technical education for the prosecution of the war seems to threaten education in the humanities, and in speech, in reports, in manifestoes, they persist in calling for help, in demanding that the humanities be "preserved," as if the humanities as we know them today were vitally important to our civilization. The true humanities are in no danger: civilization must have them, and will revive them in due course because it must have them, not because complacent professors of the false humanities are alarmed at the shrinking of their hunting preserves. Dissenting from those who show a strange lack of faith in the vitality of the humanities, President Conant, of Harvard, has wisely predicted for them "a new period of growth and evolution." But he rightly adds: "The extent and speed of this rehabilitation will depend on the imagination and statesmanship of those who now teach the liberal arts."

Granted that those who teach the liberal arts prove equal to their responsibility, they will presently give the humanities a new direction. In history, emphasis will fall on the interpretation of the best that man has done. In literature and the arts, it will fall on the best that man has said and made, and might say and make. In philosophy, it will fall on the understanding and defining of man's greatness. And in religion it will fall upon that which is greater than man.

For several centuries now, man, despite a crass cocksureness, has become less and less great in his interpretation of himself. Should this process of diminution continue, it will be idle to plan for "the great society," since the very foundation of a society, as of a person, is self-respect—well grounded self-respect. More of this belief in man has been retained by the common people than by our intellectuals. It would seem that higher education, instead of darkening or destroying this belief, should use and enlighten it.

The Realities of Our Common Life

THEODORE M. GREENE

HUMAN welfare is obviously related to human need, and the more basic the need, the more significant the welfare which arises from its satisfaction. If we survey our contemporary culture and the state of our nation today, we must agree that our greatest need is not scientific, not social, but cultural and spiritual.

Man's achievements in science during the last three hundred years have been phenomenal, and our control today over nature greatly exceeds our control over ourselves, both individually and socially. I am not suggesting that science has reached its goal, and I know that much still remains to be done, both in pure and in applied science, for our individual and national welfare. But on a comparative basis, advance in the realm of science has been far greater than in any other realm. Man's achievements in politics and economics, too, although falling far behind his achievements in the realm of science, are yet considerable. Politically, economically, and socially we have solid accomplishment to our credit.

When, however, we consider our cultural and spiritual state, the picture is not so bright. We have in large measure lost our sense of values. We have suffered from postwar disillusion. Our belief in the essential dignity of man has been impaired by our increasing failure to realize what it is that constitutes and conditions human dignity. We have lost a good portion of our cultural heritage because we have neglected to explore and assimilate it. Our religious faith is tragically weak when we consider how strong it must be if we, as a nation, are to succeed during the years to come.

As I interpret the humanities, they are the disciplines whose special responsibility it is to strengthen our sense of cultural, moral, and spiritual values. Before discussing the nature of the humanities in some detail, I should like to suggest what seems to me to be a major premise of all serious work in the humanities. I mention this premise because it has been repudiated by a philosophy of life which is still popular, though less popular today than in recent years. The premise is this: that in some sense aesthetic, moral, and religious values have an objective character. In some significant sense there are such things as works of art awaiting our study and enjoyment; there are objective moral standards which men, as men, should recognize and obey; there is a divine principle which we in the Christian tradition conceive of as a real existent Divine Being.

The objective reality of beauty and its concrete embodiments, of goodness and its impact on human life, of God and His relation to man, is the major premise of the humanistic disciplines. Deny this premise and you make thoughtful, reflective study of the arts and literatures, of morality and religion, meaningless and impossible. Such denial condemns us to a relativism in which every man's judgment is exactly as good or as bad as the judgment of anyone else, a relativism in which it is meaningless to say that we have at our disposal a rich cultural and spiritual heritage, that is, an accumulation of insights and achievements in the realm of the spirit from which we could and should benefit. To deny the objectivity of that with which the humanities are primarily concerned is to undercut all significant humanistic enterprise.

Accepting this major premise as valid, what do we mean by the humanities? Considered in terms of subject matter they concern themselves with the arts and literatures, with man's moral and religious experiences and the objects of these experiences, and with the more inclusive historical and philosophical perspective in terms of which alone the insights expressed in art and literature and the insights of morality and religion can be at all adequately understood.

We can also approach the humanities profitably in a way which some may find uncongenial and perhaps old-fashioned. But perhaps this old-fashioned approach is so old-fashioned today that it is rapidly becoming the new, the revolutionary, the really progressive approach. I refer to the disciplinary character of the humanities. The humanities can and should be described as involving a number of related disciplines.

All the humanities depend, first, upon linguistic discipline, if the term "linguistic" be taken broadly and inclusively. A training in the humanities is a training in the languages, verbal and artistic, with the aid of which men have reflected upon values, recorded their insights in the realm of values, and communicated with one another regarding objective values. One of the tragedies of American education today is the considerable failure of our students, for one reason or another, to master those languages which they must master in order to achieve an understanding of their cultural heritage, and in order to be articulate and to communicate with one another on these matters. The humanities must attempt to make good this failure by providing students with a linguistic discipline.

Second, the humanities are exploratory disciplines. They involve a mastery of all the techniques necessary to the exploration of fact, because values, as we know them, are never merely disembodied values, but are values embodied in our world of fact. Aesthetic values have their locus in works of art, which, in turn, are facts in the historical matrix. Moral values have their locus in human beings who exist in history. Religious values in all the great religions have been, in one way or another, incarnational, and in our Christian tradition, uniquely incarnational. This means that education in the humanities is a discipline in fact finding and factual interpretation. I fail to see how a person can be said to have received a sound humanistic education who is not factually informed and trained in the art of finding new facts and interpreting these facts wisely, critically, and shrewdly.

In the third place, the humanities are disciplines in sensitive appreciation. Man is so made that he is capable of aesthetic creation and response. As a human being he craves friendship and love and is capable of respect for moral values and a sense of duty. He is endowed with a deep-seated hunger for a religious anchorage, that is, a natural religious impulse. But all these innate capacities need cultivation and training. One of the functions of the humanities is therefore to sharpen our aesthetic, moral, and religious sensitivities—our capacities for imaginative insight into moral, aesthetic, and religious values.

Fourth, the humanities are disciplines in wise reflection. I mean not reflection in the narrow sense of solving particular immediate problems, but seeing any particular problem in its proper perspective. This perspective, in turn, is always a dual perspective, partly historical and partly systematic or philosophical. For there are two and only two ways in which things can be related to one another—in time, and in terms of similarity, difference, and systematic interrelationship.

The historical perspective is quite essential for any understanding of the past in its relation to the present, of the present in its relation to the past, and of the future in its relation to both the past and the present. Our young people are eager to be modern, and this desire is surely commendable. But all too often they merely succeed in being contemporary. We cannot help being contemporary if we are alive today. But to be modern is to see the present in the context of the past, and the future in terms of both the past and the present. Our students who lack the historical perspective achieve not modernity of outlook but only contemporaneity; and this means that since the immediate present quickly slips into the past, they are forever getting out of date.

Again, one of the humanistic disciplines which has fallen on evil days of late is the discipline of philosophy. I think we philosophers are largely to blame for the ineffectiveness of much contemporary philosophy. But the fact remains that unless we have some training, some discipline, in viewing things systematically in their relation to one another—morality in its relation to religion, both in their relation to art and literature, all three in their relation to science, and all humane insights and activities in their relation to social organization and corporate action—we remain essentially and necessarily provincial. We see the first with a myopia that blinds us to its true character; we cannot truly comprehend it in isolation or judge and evaluate it wisely in its relation to a larger whole.

Since it is a primary function of the humanities to make men wise, since wisdom is the product of reflection, and since reflection involves a synthesis of these two great essential perspectives—the historical and the sytematic or philosophic—it follows that discipline in wise reflection is a necessary part of humanistic education.

Finally, the humanities can and should provide a discipline in reflective commitment. This is the aspect of formal education which has perhaps been most neglected during recent years. We have come to think of the "academic" attitude as one of endless investigation and argument without decision or commitment—of never making up one's mind on anything, of never taking sides on anything, of never committing oneself to anything. This conception of the academic is one from which we must seek to free ourselves, especially in the humanistic disciplines.

When we look at the world we live in today, we see, on the one hand, large groups of people committing themselves quickly, shortsightedly, emotionally, and unreflectively, sometimes in the name of religion, sometimes in the name of patriotism, sometimes in the name of other social loyalties. And when we look at our colleges and universities, we too often find the opposite—endless reflection without sufficient recognition of the need for commitment on intellectual and spiritual questions. The humanities, if they are to accomplish what they should as human and humane activities, must educate students in the techniques of reflective commitment. The successful surgeon is a fine example of such reflective commitment. When a competent surgeon is confronted with a critical case requiring an immediate operation, he quickly marshals all the available medical knowledge bearing upon this particular problem. As an intelligent man, he knows perfectly well that all the evidence is not yet in, that the science of medicine knows only a fragment of all there is to know, that the best decision he can make may well be a wrong decision. But he also knows that he must make a decision, as reflectively as possible, but boldly and without hesitation. Were he to adopt the typical "academic" attitude (in the bad sense), his patient would die before he ever got around to him. What the surgeon actually does is to decide and act reflectively, resolutely, and courageously, fully aware of his own finitude and of all the risks involved.

We, both as individuals and as a nation, need more than anything else, perhaps, education in this kind of reflective commitment. Many students in Princeton have said to me, "If you can guarantee that, if we go into this war, the result will be a permanent and abiding peace, then we will be glad to go in." Who can guarantee a thing like that? Finite and fallible mortals must take chances. This necessity does not justify blind, emotional, impulsive action; it does justify commitment—commitment in all humanistic thought and endeavor, whether in fine art or literature, in historical or philosophical interpretation, in morals or religion.

I would suggest, then, that a student who has received a sound, enlightened humanistic education will be prepared for life with a fine linguistic equipment, a trained ability to examine facts critically, a sharpened and heightened sensitivity to values, a developed capacity for historical and philosophical reflection, and, as a culminative result of all these disciplines, an enhanced capacity for reflective decision and action.

In the light of this analysis, what are we to say in answer to the question, "What is the contribution of the humanities to our national welfare?" Our national welfare is the welfare of our democratic society, and a democratic society is to be distinguished from a totalitarian society by its peculiar recognition of the rights and duties of the individual. We in our democracy refuse to exalt the state above the individual or to think of the individual as a mere pawn. Consequently, anything that contributes essentially to the welfare of the individual contributes to our national welfare. Since the humanities are essential to the enrichment of the life of the individual and to his spiritual maturity, they contribute immeasurably to our total national welfare.

But we can also consider the problem of national welfare in more corporate terms. We can think of individuals not only as individuals, but also as citizens. What, then, are the essential conditions of effective citizenship in a democracy such as ours? Only that democracy is strong and resolute in which the individual citizens are reasonably literate and articulate, reasonably informed, reasonably endowed with a sense of objective values, capable of at least some perspective, and therefore capable in their duties as citizens of reasonably reflective commitment.

If these are the basic requirements for useful and effective citizenship, it is not easy to distinguish between that type of education which is most advantageous to the individual as an individual and that which is most advantageous to the individual as a citizen in democracy. I do not believe there is any such thing as a unique and distinctive course of study in citizenship. It may be possible perhaps to devise courses in some schools, colleges, and universities which, in a time like this, profitably focus upon some factual information and some attitudes that need emphasis in the institution in question. But, in general, education for democracy and education for citizenship are, so far as I can see, identical with the best liberal education which the individual is able to acquire.

What is the nature of the present crisis? Its surface manifestations are military, and it is our military needs which are most urgent and immediate today. Yet we all know that the military conflict reflects underlying political and economic difficulties which must be solved if peace, when it comes, is to endure. Underlying these economic, social, and political difficulties, in turn, there is the stratum of cultural values and modes of thought; our crisis is in a very real sense a cultural crisis. Finally, underlying this cultural level is the still more profound level of spiritual commitment and religious faith. The crisis in which we are all involved is, in ultimate terms, a religious crisis. That means, it seems to me, that the humanities, having to do so essentially with man's cultural and spiritual life, should make, and can make, and must make a unique contribution to our national welfare.

The Burden of Humanism

ABRAHAM FLEXNER

I PROPOSE to consider in these pages the peculiar burden laid upon humanism by developments that are nonhumanistic in their essential character. It is the merest truism to say that the outstanding features of modern life are science, industry, and democracy. Obviously, within the limits of a chapter I cannot discuss all three. I shall discuss science and humanism somewhat fully, industry and humanism briefly; democracy and humanism I cannot touch at all.

May I ask you to note, as I begin, that I am speaking of science, industry, humanism—not, in the first place, of the scientist, the industrialist, the humanist; of them, as persons, I shall have something to say as I proceed; but my immediate concern is not with persons, but with great movements in the realm of thought and action.

Science, as science, deliberately limits its range of interest. It is concerned with phenomena, concerned to collect data, to ascertain relationships, to interpret, logically and imaginatively, what it has thus gathered. Here, then, is one essential limitation to its scope: its exclusive preoccupation with data and their interpretation. There is still another, that is even more germane to my theme. Science is a two-edged sword. It is capable of doing harm as well as good, and science, as science, cannot, must not, ask which is likely to result. For example: science has had its repercussions throughout the entire range of human activities, affecting our thinking as well as our doing; it has largely—alas, not yet wholly—destroyed the puny notions within which religion, philosophy, and history respectively once led a relatively easy intellectual existence. With no more knowledge than was available two hundred years ago, one could and generally did regard the physical world as a tight little box or ball, four thousand years old—and that notion suited well the mental indolence to which men are prone. So, again, within the same little ball, ethics and philosophy were relatively easy; a historian could within prison walls write a history of the world—Sir Walter Raleigh did it—and a physician could prescribe his nostrums without scepticism, because he was so largely ignorant of the make-up and workings of the human body and the impotence of his drugs. These are, I say, puny things; and science has done well to destroy them by enlarging the scope of human knowledge, human effort, human thought, human imagination. The fortunate ones who heard Professor Shapley's Halley Lecture will realize how science has given wings to the human spirit: the endeavor to reach the poles by sled or airplane or to climb Mt. Everest is not to be despised; but it is child's play compared with that adventuring into the infinite, in space and in thought, upon which astronomy, physiology, and mathematics have for several centuries been embarked.

But while, on the one hand, science is, without making this its object, thus freeing the human spirit, it is also ministering with absolute impartiality to the worst that is within us. Physical chemistry reveals unbelievable force within the atom: it is to physical chemistry immaterial whether the outcome is a new philosophy of creation or hideous instruments of destruction for the next war. That is no business of physical chemistry; its business is to go on unraveling secrets. Every discovery that comes out of the laboratory is, as a matter of fact, seized upon simultaneously by persons who make good use of it and by persons who make the worst possible use of it. Science has brought the world closely together, for ill as for good. It has made human life safer and longer, for good and for ill; it has enabled more people to live, for good and for ill; it has introduced labor-saving devices and speed, for good and for ill; it has got rid of pestilence and infection, for good and for ill—for the bacteriology which has destroyed typhoid in peaceful cities has made possible war on a previously undreamed-of scale. It has all but destroyed quiet and solitude—for the good, perhaps, of the lonely settler, but assuredly to the detriment of the thinker who needs calm and repose, and of those who could once refresh mind and body in the silent depths of the Canadian "bush" or on the edge of an Alpine glacier. On the whole, mankind has doubtless gained—gained greatly. Science assumes that, in the long run, its success will be beneficent. But this is a very general assumption, anterior to all scientific effort whatsoever, and not pertinent to any particular activity or undertaking. Moreover, that assumption once made, it must be laid aside; it cannot be suffered to influence specific doings. Science goes its way, dealing now with this problem, now with that, regardless of proximate use or ultimate bearing. It is no concern of science as such that the diplomatist, businessman, warrior, statesman, or inventor may, thanks to it, perpetrate or scheme atrocities from which, objectively viewed, every sane and civilized person recoils. Nor does science deserve any credit for the optimistic interpretation which a humanitarian age has placed upon the doctrine of evolution. That, as Santayana says in *Reason in Science*, "is a notion that has nothing to do with natural science."

Scientific method, in the sense in which I have been discussing it, is as valid in the field of humanism as in the realm of physics or biology; indeed the Germans have a single word—*Wissenschaft*—covering both. For humanism must, like natural science, procure data, generalize, interpret. Painstaking, sometimes monumental, works bear witness to the efforts of humanism to obtain accurate data: historic sites are excavated to procure the contemporaneous records and relics of ancient events; manuscripts are deciphered and compared; inscriptions are copied and photographed; dust-covered archives are searched. Work of this kind corresponds in the field of humanism to the scientific endeavor to observe phenomena; it is, in the proper sense of the term, scientific—the search for facts in the realm of the human spirit upon which generalization, hypothesis, interpretation may safely rest. A library is a laboratory. Philology in the technical sense is science, not humanism. The intellectual processes operating in excavating below ground are precisely the same as those operating in the observation of the heavens. Moreover, both humanistic and scientific studies have often suffered in the same way from inadequacy of data, from erroneous observation, from premature generalization, from unjustified interpretation. As Duclaux, the author of *Pasteur—The History of a Mind*, wrote, "A series of judgments, revised without ceasing, goes to make up the incontestable progress of science. We must believe in progress, but we must never accord more than a limited amount of confidence to the forms in which it is successively vested." This statement is equally true of pathology and history. Both tend to run in grooves, out of which only giants have been able to lift them, for there are fashions and patterns, difficult to change, in the natural sciences, as in literature, history, politics, or art.

In revulsion from the easy interpretations of previous generations, the scientific side of humanistic studies has therefore in the last century been strongly emphasized. This has been thoroughly sound procedure. In humanism as in science men had gone too far on the basis of insufficient data. They had, and they still have, to address themselves to the task of learning the facts about man and his spiritual productions with all possible accuracy and fullness and with total disregard of consequences to established beliefs, customs, or practices. There is therefore a science of history, a science of Assyriology, as impartially devoted to just finding things out as the science of physics. In deciphering an inscription or subjecting the Bible to textual criticism, humanism has as little concern for consequences as geology when it unearths fossils that upset the Book of Genesis, or chemistry which is ultimately responsible for the use of gas in warfare.

I have just said that science and humanism face the same perils in the interpretation of data. The biographers of Pasteur, to whom I shall have occasion to recur, quite candidly show that he was sometimes wrong about facts and correct in his inferences, occasionally right about facts and wrong in his inferences, even though usually, in the end, as far as he went, right as to both. But the point is that, using not only judgment but imagination, he had to interpret as well as unravel—the mere accumulation of data is insufficient—and that he could go wrong in either adventure or in both. Humanistic studies face the same problem, even though the humanistic problem be more complex, as human beings and human society are more complex than atoms, bacteria, and stellar systems. For humanism, like science, has not only to describe, it has to interpret beyond the point at which details stop, though, as in science, that point is being steadily pushed forward. To take examples from history: Cromwell and Napoleon and Lincoln and Bismarck and Lenin were results of specific antecedent causes and factors, many of which can be definitely ascertained; but assuredly antecedents, opportunities, conditions cannot yet be formulated in terms that would satisfy a biologist or even a psychologist—not to say a physicist or chemist; again, they produced results—but results that depended in each case on individuality—on a peculiar type of intelligence, moral sense, ambition, purpose, wit, will—that are thus far indescribable. They had not only social and environmental histories that may be quite adequately portrayed—see, for example, Sandburg's account of the prairie years of Abraham Lincoln—but they have each histories, family and individual, social, psychological, physiological, and anatomical. The results of the impact when an individual of unknown idiosyncrasies— a Socrates, Shakespeare, Napoleon, or Lincoln—crashes into history require interpretation, but with great risks. The current of events, which has been moving in a certain channel, is suddenly and incalculably wrenched from its course; thus the emergence and consequences of personality are with our present resources for investigation to a considerable extent accidental. And what is true in history is still more true of literature, art, music—of the Homers and Shakespeares and Goethes and Heines, of Michelangelo and Bach and Wagner, whom up to a certain point one can account for—but who, beyond that point, are, as far as our present powers of analysis and expression go, still mysteries, inexplicable and unpredictable. Wit and technique are gradually narrowing this realm; but we have as yet far to go in eliminating the imponderable from the humanistic as from the scientific field.

I mentioned industry as characteristic of the modern age. Industry, mere industry, industry as such, is primarily concerned in satisfying needs or in creating needs that its products may satisfy. It is a fine thing when its activities give improved shelter, clothing, food, abolish famine and even the danger of famine. Like science, industry is entitled to the assumption that on the whole its activities are beneficent. None the less, industry, qua industry, is engaged in making profits. Hence industry, which, like science, has plainly accomplished so much that is good, has always been more or less ruthless—at one time frankly so, nowadays sometimes more subtly. The same business activities, that have made food and clothing cheap or accessible, and that once exploited children in factories, now make peons of African natives and thoughtlessly destroy Oxford's superbly beautiful countryside. Since the last war, as the Slade Professor of Fine Arts exclaims, "We have built a million houses; at how many of those can we look without shame and disgust?" Niagara is hopelessly disfigured by the base uses to which paint and electricity have been put. Sitting in a railway carriage on the Continent, I once overheard an American lady upbraid Germans, because the Germans, like other Europeans, permit women to do the hard work of the fields—to plough, to harvest, to tend the cattle, regardless of the weather. The German lady responded: "Do you really think these women out here in the open, enjoying sun and sky and air, would be better off operating a cotton machine, in a hot factory, with thousands of others, similarly occupied in a deadening, mechanical routine?" Industry does not as industry ask these embarrassing questions. It produces, produces, produces; distributes, distributes, distributes; advertises, advertises, advertises; silk and shoddy; tinsel and gems. Ours is the age of the machine; and the machine, as machine, is efficient, not sensitive. Indeed, the well-being of a given society, even the vigor of humanistic studies, may today depend indirectly upon mass production, well distributed in the world's markets.

It is therefore plain that neither the unraveling of Nature's secrets nor the application of knowledge to practical ends carries us as far as we are impelled to go. The passion for knowledge as such—any sort of knowledge—is, of course, as pure a passion as human beings are capable of indulging. But when every riddle due to ignorance has been solved, and all the facts about all phenomena are known and applied, what then? The accumulation of information, the knowledge of relationships, the industrial application of knowledge to practical ends of one kind or another must be appraised. Within science itself, within industry itself, there is neither apparatus nor inclination to appraise what science and industry do. And there must not be. The thoroughness and impartiality of science would suffer, if its task were complicated by the necessity of thinking of the worth or use of what it is doing; it is its task to find things out, and there its task, qua science, ends.

If science and industry are held down to their essential part, it becomes clear that somewhere a rational system of values must be developed, outside science as such, outside industry as such, and yet ultimately operative within both. It is this sense of value that will make distinctions and thus determine the direction of human development. The assessment of values, in so far as human beings are affected, constitutes the unique burden of humanism. Science, I have said, is concerned with the phenomena, with happenings—in the remotest fixed stars, on our own planet, within our own bodies, in our personal and social relations. But while the task of the scientist, as scientist, leaves him there, the completed task of the humanist carries him farther. Sooner or later the humanist, as humanist, must concern himself with worthwhileness; he must raise the question of value, not only in the particular field in which he operates scientifically, but elsewhere. There is no moment at which the scientist, as scientist, calls the law of gravitation reasonable or absurd; he is indifferent as to the beneficence of atoms or germs. He asks, "Is this true?," not, "Is this beautiful or good?" He is satisfied when he understands and ceases to be puzzled. Not so the humanist. He must, to be sure, understand, as best he can; but, beyond this, he cannot ultimately help—it is inherent in the very word "humanism"—distinguishing between the beautiful and the ugly, the noble and the base, the farsighted and the immediate, the serene quiet of the depths, and the noisy and meaningless tumult of the surface. The humanist has nothing to tell the scientist about science; indeed, as I have pointed out, in one important aspect of his own work he takes a leaf out of the scientist's book. But whenever consequences ensue and action results, humanism rightly intervenes. Is this good or bad? Beautiful or ugly? Wholesome or unwholesome? Worthwhile or not worthwhile? Broad or narrow? These are questions that humanism cannot avoid. It is hopelessly lost, if prejudice influences or abbreviates the initial investigation of facts, creations, and situations; it falls short, if it is ultimately without concern about them, and from this point of view the applications of science are answerable to the humanistic spirit. The physicist lays bare facts and relations which the inventor ingeniously turns to use. The facts and relations are per se valuable; is the invention—telephone, subway, motorboat, what not? It is the interpreter of ideals who must tentatively answer "yes" and "no." Are these worthwhile? The humanist answers both "yes" and "no." Yes, in so far as labor and sheer difficulty are reduced, in order that men may be freed to love, think, meet, cooperate, associate, enjoy; no, in so far as mere speed and noise have been converted into human obsessions. An amusing and significant story illustrating the point is told of the late Dr. Booker T. Washington, the great Negro, who founded Tuskegee Institute. Dr. Washington tried to keep in touch with his former pupils by visiting them from time to time on their farms and in their homes. On one occasion, a former student, exhibiting to his revered leader a model pigpen, explained that he had discovered that, if corn were first softened in hot water, a pig could digest it in half the time. Dr. Washington's quick comment—"What's a pig's time worth anyway?"—went to the heart of the whole speed craze. What's it worth anyway? In this age of increasing complications—more movement, more comfort, more contact, more books, more business, more territory, more people, more students, more money, more of this, that, and everything, the question has got to be put insistently and courageously, "What's it worth to mankind anyway?" And the humanistic spirit must answer.

I have tried to point out, first, that as fact-gathering and interpreting activities, science and humanism are one; further, that, sooner or later, humanism must do what science as science does not do—it must raise questions of relative or actual value, beauty, wholesomeness. Now science and humanism take concrete form in persons; and persons are neither simple nor single-minded. Persons try to be whole, try—or should try—in different moods or for different purposes to detach themselves from one attitude and to embrace another. Scientists and humanists alike have, as persons, preferences, interests, and capacities that belong to various categories. The scientist, having emerged from his laboratory, may allow his humanistic instinct to have play; the humanist has not gone to the limit unless it has played. That, I think, marks a genuine distinction.

The necessary detachment and indifference of science can best be realized through the study of some supreme scientific intelligence. Pasteur lends himself admirably to this study. His life is an open book; its events have been admirably recounted by his biographer, his son-in-law, Vallery-Radot; the history of his mind has been clearly traced by Duclaux, his pupil and successor. Pasteur was a decidedly complex personality: an intensely patriotic Frenchman, concerned alike for the glory and the material prosperity of his country; so sensitive that he could scarcely endure the thought of experimentation upon animals; endowed with imagination, the value and the danger of which he well knew; in the depths of his nature, profoundly religious. Yet he was above all a scientist, bent upon ascertaining the truth; and in so far as truth was concerned, everything else was, for the time being, nonexistent for him. It is interesting to observe that one whose doings transformed important industries and wrought unspeakable blessings to suffering mankind was not originally interested in either prosperity or health. He saw in course of time—in some instances he foresaw—the medical, humanitarian, and economic implications of his work. But these were not his primary concern. "A disease, as a disease, did not interest him deeply. . . . That which interested him was the pathological conflict between the properties of the micro-organism and of the cells of the tissues." Pasteur's insatiable scientific curiosity was both prior to and independent of his patriotic and humanitarian impulses.

Something similar happens in industry. Consciously or unconsciously the medieval craftsman was a humanist, not a merchant or a manufacturer; he cared nothing for mass production; he created works of art. But, quite obviously, he fitted only into an unscientific and an undemocratic age; most people simply "went without." Science and democracy introduce an era when everybody wants things and can get them. They are produced cheaply and in enormous quantity by the machine. That is the motivation alike of Manchester and Grand Rapids. I leave the humanitarian to deal with the ethical and sanitary problems created by the factory; the burden of the humanist is increased by the necessity of contributing an aesthetic value to its products. Industry, like science, is thus answerable to standards and ideals which lie outside and beyond it and which it is the concern of the humanist, now and then in the person of the industrialist himself, to create and to apply. It is interesting to observe the extent to which the humanistic spirit has invaded the factory. Many examples could be cited: let me give two or three. An artist in wrought iron—Brandt—has shown in Paris that the factory can turn out an abundant and a beautiful product: Mr. Henry Creange, French by birth, American by adoption, has shown that the demand of an almost insatiable market for silk can be satisfied as tastefully with the huge output of the factory as by the craftsmen of Lyons. Mass production has quite destroyed the art of printing. A few craftsmen have, however, arisen in the new world as in the old, who are endeavoring to conquer the refractory press. One of them, Mr. R. W. Chapman, in his *Portrait of a Scholar*, an exquisite little volume written on the battlefields of Macedonia, described with perhaps excessive modesty the early steps of the humanistic conquest: "It is a melancholy and humiliating truth that the history of printing is a long decadence. Even in the mechanics of printing we cannot today surpass the pioneers of the fifteenth century. We cannot achieve a finer paper or a cleaner impression. Our best types are modelled on theirs; and in the use of our tools, in all the rules of the art, we toil painfully in their wake. A great scholar and accomplished collector used to say that his study of early printing had cured him of the vulgar

Radicalism of his youth. The early printers had the tradition of the scribes in their souls, and so the new art found its perfection at a spring. It has been in a slow decline for four centuries; and the best that we can do now is to follow the old models, and adapt the old methods, with what intelligence we may command."

The industrial museum, which began in Germany and is gradually spreading over the Western world, represents an effort to merge into the consumer, who, as such, merely wants goods, and the manufacturer, who, as such, wants merely to make and to profit by them, the humanist who holds that things shall have meaning and beauty as well as use.

The distinction which exists between science and humanism is thus capable of being softened, even turned to advantage within the realm of industry. For the humanist may, as I have pointed out, not only affect industry; the industrialist may in the process of humanizing his operations promote the primary ends of industry. Photography, building, engineering may accomplish their primary purposes all the better, all the more profitably, by being sensitive to aesthetic considerations. On the other hand, they can never lose sight of the limits within which industry must operate: for on the whole and in the long run industry must pay. The specter of the market is always there; education may drive it back; it cannot be exorcised. Industry cannot be humanized to the point at which its products are so lovely or its methods so humane as to result in bankruptcy.

The sources of the criteria which the humanist applies are not transcendental; they lie, according to my thinking, deep in the human soul. Humanistic authority springs from human tradition, human reflection, human reason. I do not close my eyes to the difficulties arising from differences of taste. But, somehow, in the progress of time, though a permanent dead level is never attained, the wheat is separated from the chaff, and ideals, while remaining personal, attain the quality of not being merely our own transient selves. *These ideals are in the special custody of the humanist*, however often he has himself fallen short in range of sympathy and understanding. He may not be dogmatic in applying them, for they are not immutable and he may err; but with all respect and deference, it is his task to see things in perspective, to measure tentatively the work and doings of the human spirit, scientific, practical, and humanistic as well. To be sure, the oftener a humanistic strain is present in the scientist, or the businessman, the better; I am not suggesting that the professional humanist can alone possess good taste. There have been humanists whose methods were highly scientific but whose taste was execrable. But my point is that the roundly developed humanist is necessarily concerned with meaning and beauty, whereas the scientist has, as scientist, to be careful not to become entangled in either. And the extent to which applied science and industry and human life in general are significant and attractive may depend on the authority which humanistic studies are able to obtain. "The teacher of literature," Professor Lowes of Harvard once wrote to me, "ought to have vision and imagination closely akin to the vision and imagination of a poet, for he has to transmute the raw materials of scholarship into instrumentalities for the interpretation of an art. The qualities which he must exercise in acquisition are the qualities which attach to rigorous scientific method; but the faculties brought into play in application are not so much the faculties of the scientist as of the artist."

That the humanist must assess values would, I assume, be universally admitted in reference to antiquity. No one questions that it is the proper concern of the humanist not only to understand Confucius and Homer and Plato and Cicero and Erasmus, but to interpret, appreciate, and appraise them and the civilization out of which they sprang. With similar objectivity and lack of personal interest historians record and judge the doings of peoples, of Assyrians, Egyptians, Hebrews,

Greeks, Latins, Huns, and the various medieval nations. Is the case different when modern or contemporary nations, personages, or events are in question? Of course, the past looks easier. Is the difference as marked as appears? Is it not perhaps simplified for us by ignorance and imagination? To be sure, time, the inexorable humanist, has done deadly work. The flimsy building has collapsed; the demagogue has been shown up; the poor colors have faded; the meretricious lyric has ceased to charm. But difficulties enough remain. Adequate data are almost never obtainable; pitfalls, due to mere ignorance, beset every inch of the road; current prejudices may even influence judgment.

The humanist, dealing with the contemporary world, faces other problems. He may not lack information, but he does lack perspective; and his feelings are less easily discounted. Nevertheless, the abundance of available data, the possibility of first-hand knowledge of men, books, opinions, social conditions, give him tremendous advantages. Of these opportunities, the scholar is sometimes slow—often too slow—to take advantage. Perhaps the conservatism of the university atmosphere is responsible for his timidity. In any event, a German writing of Shakespeare sees him against a narrower background than when he writes of Homer or Plato; when the Englishman writes of Goethe, he deals with a great man, a great author, with contracted grasp of the picture. The closer one comes to our own times and our own people, the narrower, the more particularistic, humanistic studies tend to become. One easily forgets one is English or German or American when one writes of Egypt or Troy; one does not readily forget it, and few try to forget it, when writing of recent events, current topics, or current literature.

The perfect humanist, qua humanist, would not fear to appraise Gilbert and Sullivan as objectively as he appraises Aristophanes; he would be as little excited about Bolshevism and Socialism, Protestantism and Catholicism, as he is about

Guelph and Ghibelline, Cavalier and Roundhead, slaveholder and abolitionist. The living author must be seen, larger or smaller, against the background of his nation's and humanity's achievement; the living statesman must get his stature by comparison with Pericles and Caesar; current events must be ranged beside the already historic comedies and the tragedies for which useless wars have been waged, useless horrors endured, useless sacrifices made. The final panorama of Childe Roland need not be postponed until the present has become part and parcel of antiquity:

> There they stood, ranged along the hill-sides, met
>> To view the last of me, a living frame
>> For one more picture! in a sheet of flame
> I saw them and I knew them all. And yet
> Dauntless the slug-horn to my lips I set,
>> And blew.

Endeavors of the kind I am now discussing belong under modern conditions to universities. As a matter of fact, the past cannot really be comprehended without them; but regardless of the past, they are appropriate to universities, just because universities have no responsibility for action or policy, but complete responsibility for ascertaining, telling, and interpreting the truth—the truth in respect not only to stardust and atoms, but to pictures and poems and politicians and economic theories, present as well as past. Do what we will, we shall not correctly anticipate the judgments of time and history; but frail and faulty as we are, we can do much better than we have done or are doing. Finality is possible in neither scientific doctrine nor in humanistic evaluation; but both are necessary to progress in clearer thinking. The saturation point of fact once reached, the finished scholar may not, I think, shrink from a philosophic attempt to set a value on the subject of his study—to see it in perspective, to estimate its value; and the fact that subsequent generations may revise his judgment does not render his effort superfluous.

A few years ago I was seated at dinner next to a distinguished Oxonian. The conversation turned on the subject of books about various nations written by foreigners. "No one," said he, "but a Scot or a German can write a good book about England, and a German has done it." On inquiry I learned that my neighbor referred to a recent work, entitled *England* by Wilhelm Dibelius. A few weeks later I met Dibelius himself in Berlin, talked with him about England and Germany, and procured a copy of his book. I have no opinion as to the qualifications one must possess in order to do justice to the English people. But the substance of the preface to this study of England made upon me a profound impression. It keeps on recurring to me: "Germany has been at war with a people whom Germany did not understand and who did not understand Germany." In the century or half-century preceding the war, what did the humanists of the great English, German, French, and American universities do to appraise these nations and to interpret them to one another? Perhaps in any case their efforts would have been vain; perhaps business and dynasties and newspapers and politicians and soldiers and seamen, working in the grooves in which men work, would nevertheless have steered the whole civilized world upon the rocks, uncertain when or whether it would be seaworthy again. But in any event humanists might have had clear consciences. They are not now entitled to them. Goethe was studied in England, Shakespeare in Germany and France; but the larger issues were ignored, left to practical men. I am not supposing that the humanist must be denationalized; I am only asking that he take as broad and as critical a view of modern life and culture as he takes of ancient life and culture; that he should not wait a century or two until the present has faded into antiquity before trying to be judicial, before trying to interest himself in the whole of a given civilization. As it turned out, professors everywhere were little broader than Nelson's captain, who is reported to have said, "My lord, I have not prejudices, but God knows I hate a Frenchman."

Plato suggests that the world had better be governed by scholars, but, as I have already pointed out, scholars may be influential, precisely because they have no responsibility for policies. They occupy for this reason a peculiarly strong position; their interest is in interpretation and evaluation and not merely in particularistic facts or laws; the world might therefore conceivably be governed by wiser and better men, if in the universities, through which most of the governors and many of the governed pass, a group of men, caring about values, expounded truth rather than glory; if professors of German and French and Spanish and English were human beings—humanists—before or besides being Germans, Frenchmen, Spaniards, Englishmen, or Americans. In that case, the world would not care less for science than it does or should care—for it is far from caring enough; but its actual fate would not be so largely committed to practical men who care altogether too little for science, still less for humanism, and altogether too much for the uses, individual or nationalistic, to which exploited science and industry can be put.

I am urging, as you will perceive, a broader, deeper, and more fearless conception of humanistic studies—urging that, without interfering with the specialized or scientific interests of the archeologist, the paleographer, or the historian, humanism should, further, charge itself with the appreciation of the present as well as of the past, of the value of science, of the value of industry, of the soundness, comprehensiveness, justice, fairness, worthwhileness of government, ours, yours, other nations'. Scholars are prone to take pride in withdrawing from the world of their own day; they let it alone; and the world is, in my opinion, much the worse for that.

The claim of a larger scope for humanistic enterprise goes hand in hand with vigorous encouragement of science and industry. It is idle to rail against either. The world went bankrupt on sheer ignorance of fact. Inevitably the pendulum swung in the opposite direction. We have therefore entered upon an era of science, mechanism, machine-production, with all the social and aesthetic consequences and problems therein involved. No merely pedantic, antiquarian, intolerant, resistant, or unsympathetic type of humanism is going successfully to impose a scheme of values on the tremendous energy that is being released. With mounting zeal men have sought to know more and to use what they find out; with utter naïveté the responsibility for government has been devolved upon the masses. As a matter of fact, though knowledge and democracy have both achieved obvious triumphs in both intellectual and social realms, neither from knowledge as such, nor from democracy as such, does salvation spontaneously come: salvation is a thing of the spirit, a thing of purpose, a thing of value. The ultimate control of the physical and social forces which the last two centuries have released depends therefore on an assertive humanistic spirit; and among the assertive humanists one must, as I have already intimated, count not only the professional humanist—he may not even belong to the number—but any person—scientist, statesman, or layman—who, divesting himself of his prejudice or prepossessions, surveys his work and that of others from the standpoint of its value to civilization.

Of the teaching of modern subjects, it can, I think, be fairly said that thus far literature, language, and history have been largely viewed as ends in themselves and but rarely as means for that profound sympathy and comprehension which Dibelius seeks.

The history of the Taylor Institution, like the history of all modern subjects, shows the obstacles encountered by the development of humanism. It is only within the last twenty-odd years—too late to count yet for much in its effect on present-day affairs—that this institution, devoted to the teaching of modern languages and literatures, has notably expanded; even for this limited function, its facilities are sadly inadequate. What is one to say of the capacity of other university departments at Oxford and elsewhere to extend their scope, so that nations, which are becoming increasingly interdependent, may not only know of one another's masterpieces in literature or art, may not only seek at one and at the same time to promote trade and intercourse, but really to understand one another? No modern university in any country is, as far as I know, equipped properly to undertake this larger function; nowhere could the effort be more hopefully made than at Oxford, which educates so large a proportion of the Englishmen who govern the Empire, its dominions, and dependencies, and, perhaps most important of all, are the means of communication between the Empire and foreign nations.

And it is not only with respect to foreign nations that the humanist will be fearless and candid; it may be more difficult, but it is assuredly not impossible to be objective with respect to one's own nation. It can no longer be left to superficial travelers to give their hasty and misleading judgments of other peoples— usually playing up to their own inborn nationalistic preferences; nor can it be left to the hundred per cent German, Frenchman, Englishman, or American to value his own nation and thus confirm the unthinking in their native prejudices. What Bryce in his day did for the United States, what Dibelius has done for England, English, American, French, and German scholars must endeavor to do for their own, as for other, countries. That is the burden that rests upon the shoulders of humanism in a world that will become a chaos if men do not strive to understand both themselves and one another.

To the preceding discussion it may, I think, be fairly objected that it has kept too closely to what Mr. Graham Wallas has called the "anthropomorphic plane": it has tried to analyze and to conceive abstractly the working scientist, the working humanist. I have done this in order to bring into sharper relief the importance of appraisal detached from the mere search for knowledge or its application. Now let me, in concluding, add that there come supreme moments to the rare genius—philosopher, scientist, poet—to Plato, Newton, Descartes, Einstein—when, in the white heat of intellectual and spiritual passion, all distinctions melt away, when philosopher, scientist, and artist are one. It is not without significance that an English poet, searching for expression adequate to his ecstasy, found it in the rapture of the astronomer and the explorer:

> Then felt I like some watcher of the skies
> When a new planet swims into his ken;
> Or like stout Cortez when with eagle eyes
> He star'd at the Pacific—and all his men
> Look'd at each other with a wild surmise—
> Silent, upon a peak in Darien.

At the level of intense feeling and deepest penetration, even human values dissolve, and things are what they are for their own sake and that alone.

Civilization and the Arts

WILLIAM MACNEILE DIXON

THE English poets and men of letters of the seventeenth and eighteenth centuries claimed for themselves a high office. It was no less a claim than to be missionaries of civilization. And what was civilization? The outcome of an effort, they would have answered, to render human society, in all possible ways open to mankind, less harassing and more agreeable, the effort to soften life's asperities, to substitute persuasion and good sense for the barbaric violence, threatenings, and slaughter by which human intercourse has in the past been so terribly disfigured, to substitute the enlightening exchange of opinions for the destructive exchange of grapeshot. It represented, in brief, simply an attempt, however unconscious, to elevate human life above material needs and preoccupations, to provide it with spiritual interests, to introduce into our short and anxious lives as much of grace and dignity as were attainable in the conditions of man's estate. In this great endeavor—so the Renaissance humanists believed—the arts in general, poetry, music, painting, sculpture, architecture, might not only be of assistance, but, setting religion aside, should prove the most promising and most potent of all available agencies. Conversely, the standard of civilization attained by any race or nation might, they held, be justly estimated by its care for these things, the place they held in the estimation of its citizens.

In a word, art and literature were not merely to be regarded as pursuits pleasant in themselves, as agreeable forms of escape from anxiety and boredom or mere ornamental additions to social intercourse, but beyond doubt the most valuable of all allies in the long battle for a nobler and a better future, as making for the common good of human society. This engaging conception found, it may be conceded, at least a firm basis in the universal interest the pursuit and practice of the arts had through historic times excited, each in its own manner and measure, among the tribes and peoples of mankind. They had everywhere and in all ages been in some fashion cultivated and in some degree enjoyed. They had met, so history seemed to report, certain deep-seated needs of human nature, and—a very revelant and significant circumstance—they had in no respect added to the distresses or tribulations of the race, never been employed as the instruments of tyranny to inflict cruelty, to support injustice, to imprison thought. The practice of these arts had never led to revolutions, massacres, or wars. Could as much be said of politics, or even of religion? They had done much for the welfare of suffering mortals, so under Renaissance influences, the humanists, poets, and men of letters contended, might they not be trusted to do much more?

So simple a faith in the efficacy of art and letters as the most powerful of all civilizing agencies wears in our time a somewhat antiquated air. It has lost something of its early charm. Its open advocates are few. We have long since transferred our allegiance to other remedies for our ills. We have put our trust in political, economic, and scientific remedies—yet, judging from the present state of the world, without any very dazzling or resounding success. The benefits conferred upon humanity by modern science are, indeed, beyond enumeration. They call for our wonder and astonishment. And who could fail to take pride in the magnificent witness it bears to the powers and resources of the human mind? Its victories have been spectacular, its successes border upon the miraculous. For some reason, nevertheless, these victories and successes do not include those for which we hoped. Wiser, no doubt, we are, yet the age of science, which made us so, has proved a disappointment. We, its children, are no happier, perhaps less happy than our predecessors. How is this? If it be so, the poets and artists need not in the

proud presence of the men of science confess themselves superfluous persons, nor altogether hide their diminished heads.

But there remains in this context a searching question not to
be ignored. However they may have served humanity in the
youth of the world, is there in an age of reason like our own,
which bows the knee in reason's shrine and knows no other
deity, any longer need of, or any future for, the arts at all? Is it
not the truth, if we can bear to hear it, that their day is done?
Absurd, you say. Yet great men have told us so, many men have
feared it. "Thought and reflection," announced Hegel, in no
uncertain voice, "have taken their flight above fine art." Ma-
caulay was not less oracular upon the matter. "As civilization
advances," he declared, "poetry almost necessarily declines."
Peacock sounded the same confident note. "When the mind
becomes more enlarged and comprehensive, as reason gains the
ascendancy over imagination and feeling, the empire of thought
is withdrawn from poetry, which can no longer accompany it
on its progress, and leaves the understanding to advance alone."
And again, "Poetry can never make a philosopher nor statesman, nor in any class of life a useful or rational man." Well, it's
a fair challenge, and should be met.

What, then, can sensibly be said for the pursuit and practice
of these arts? The order of precedence among them—a pretty
enough inquiry, if perhaps a trifle contentious—is not at the
moment in question, and the word "poetry" may fairly be employed as representative of the fine arts in general, with which
it is closely associated, with whose outlook upon human life
theirs may without demur be identified. Music and painting,
sculpture and architecture are all poetry in its widest sense. The
nobler arts are a sisterhood, and poetry may be permitted to
speak for the rhythmical family to which all belong.

Here, then, is the question. Have we now, in a world no
longer young, outgrown poetry, as children outgrow their toys?
Does the advance in knowledge toll the death knell, as Hegel

predicted, of the fine arts? Is it in sober fact possible to be so wise, so well informed as to have little or no further need of them? Are the great poets and artists of the world—assuming the comparison not wholly senseless—less trustworthy as leaders of thought, as interpreters of the universe to their fellow creatures, or of ourselves to ourselves, than the thinkers in other fields? Are they of less consequence, or of lower intellectual stature than the followers of pure reason, the men of science and the philosophers?

It is commonly assumed or believed that the arts deal in fancies rather than in facts, in flights of imagination rather than hard realities, that poetry is "a kind of ingenious nonsense," that one and all they are the occupations of idle dreamers, and that we must take counsel with men of stiffer grain, of a very different and superior order to assist us in the building of a better world. Well, is it so?

We cannot fail to observe that poets and artists are seldom included in the accredited histories of human thought. They are not usually mentioned among the profound and penetrating philosophic minds. And yet I cannot avoid asking myself, what else, if not thinking, was Cervantes doing when he wrote that wonder of wonders among books, *Don Quixote*, or Ictinus when he designed that miracle of loveliness, the Parthenon at Athens? For my part I cannot assign, let us say Euripides, to a lower intellectual rank than Hobbes or Locke, declare Beethoven less logical than Kant, or Rembrandt than John Stuart Mill. To think Michelangelo's mind less profound than Galileo's, Shakespeare's less subtle than Spinoza's seems to me a strange reversal of the truth. For the poets and artists had a talent hard to match. To their mental depth and acuteness they added an imaginative, a creative power so rare and astonishing as, on that count alone, to win the hearts of men. Comparisons are odious, and in this field also a trifle ridiculous. If made at all, it must peremptorily be said that to succeed greatly in the arts demands not less "fundamental brainwork" than in any of the higher undertakings of the mind. Within the field of pure reason and intelligence the poets and artists take, in their own manner, and by no means in an inferior manner, their rightful place with the most exact and comprehensive thinkers the world has known.

No one in his senses will attempt to diminish the glory of modern science. Let us, however, bear in mind an obvious truth. Before so much as the word "science" rose above the intellectual horizon, countless millions of human beings had passed across the great stage, lived in most respects much as we ourselves live, as perforce all must live, eating and drinking, marrying, sorrowing, rejoicing. Despite all our advantages, all our knowledge, in their day and generation it does not appear they were less happy and contented than we. The Greeks, in their most brilliant era, who attained two thousand years ago so high a pitch of culture, knew nothing of science in our understanding of it, its conveniences and blessings. Of chemistry, of astronomy, and all the rest they had not a modern schoolboy's knowledge. Physiology and pathology did not exist. Medicine and surgery were in their babyhood. Nevertheless in their absence, even in the absence of the wonderful modern inventions, Plato and Aristotle, Aeschylus and Aristophanes, Socrates and Pericles appear to have suffered little hardship, to have thought and written, carved and built as well, to say the least of it, as most men since, and in the absence of all the paraphernalia of modern education to have attained a highly respectable degree of wisdom and civility. How are we to suppose all this came about? One wonders occasionally whether our much-talked-of civilization has all the advantages our fancy paints, whether its accumulated machinery of fast and furious distractions leaves us time for thought at all, or bears any profitable relation to our inner lives.

To what conclusions, then, are we driven? Not, indeed, that

the things our forerunners lacked are worthless things—the railways, the telephones, the electric light have their value. Conclude we must, however, that a high state of civilization, define it as you will, may be attained without them. It does not consist, as some have fondly imagined, in the knowledge of nature's laws or the control of her forces. And to another inference no less certain and important: machinery cannot make a civilization. If we propose to look to science for our salvation, there is this to bear in mind. Science moves on the circumference of our lives. She has her being in the outer and physical world, as far removed from the interior region of our deepest and most intimate experiences as the northern from the southern pole.

There is, as everyone knows, a province of human life—and only upon reflection do we perceive how vast, how boundless is that province—to whose interests and problems the most extensive knowledge or control of nature's machinery affords no entrance, a country upon which the bright sun of science sheds not a ray of light. It is the country of the soul. We have our affections and sympathies, we have loves and friendships, we have hopes and fears and admirations, inmates of a province of real things as broad and deep as the telescopic heavens above our heads. Of these things science never speaks. She sits above the battle and has no share in our joys and sorrows. Of good and evil, freedom and justice, science has nothing to say. The scientific vocabulary does not include such words as beauty or heroism, nobility or charm, resignation or despair, kindness or generosity, character or conduct. Not until you ponder such words do you perceive how narrow and inhuman is the view that omits them, the interim experiences with which our minds are so continuously occupied from the cradle to the grave.

It is necessary to remind ourselves that the physical sciences exclude the humanities, and are not interested in the great pageant of the world, the rise and fall of kingdoms, the lives of great men, statesmen, martyrs, soldiers, saints, or their part in the shaping of human history, that they never so much as mention the revolutions, the wars, the religions, the mighty events in the panorama of the past? How vast, then, is the gap in the scientific program. And how fantastic to suppose, if we do suppose, that the sciences, which are by their nature excluded or exclude themselves from the province of the heart and its affections, can minister to our most urgent and deepest necessities, and, unassisted, build for us the society of our dreams. The arts, which are at home where the sciences are strangers, in the very region where logic is at a loss and the most lofty understanding ill at ease, can hardly fail to prove themselves the better guides and interpreters through the labyrinth of mankind's perplexities.

Ours is an age of crowding doubts, and among them a deep misgiving haunts the world today. It has begun to doubt the power or sufficiency of the unassisted reason to resolve its torturing problems, and of political and economic devices to meet and serve its needs. Pursued though it be through weary days and sleepless nights, the search for material remedies to soothe or cure our spiritual distresses can have only one end—failure. Much more will be needed than to feed the hungry, house the poor, clothe the destitute, however generously contrived and devotedly administered these undertakings may be. The day of acceptance of the great truth approaches, than which a greater was never yet proclaimed, that "man does not live by bread alone." With its acceptance and not till then will be laid the foundation stone of a civilization worthy the name.

Four hundred years have passed since that famous era of startling events and discoveries entitled by historians the Renaissance. We are still governed by Renaissance ways of thought, and among the heart-shaking, spirit-searching thoughts that took shape in the fourteenth and fifteenth centuries, then entered and took possession of the European mind, one new idea must be assigned pride of place, so commanding was it, so uplifting, so supreme. It was the idea of progress. The idea of a continuous, never ending advance of the human race toward a nobler and a happier world, an earthly paradise. The very thought aroused hope and stimulated effort. It provided an aim, an ideal, an adventure, a common undertaking for all mankind. This immense expectation or inspired vision, to us so familiar and so natural, had, difficult as it is to believe, never entered and had no place in the mental furniture of the medieval nor yet the ancient world. The men of earlier days entertained no such hope for themselves or the generations to come. No such sunlit, encouraging prospect had ever before been harbored on earth since creation's dawn. What wonder, then, that a conception that magnificently widened the hopes and enhanced the values of life captured the human mind? For it transformed the whole scene of existence.

How, then, do matters stand today? The Renaissance had two sides. It displayed itself in an enthusiasm for the newly discovered classical civilization in its brilliant achievements; it displayed itself also in the spirit of scientific inquiry. To which, if any comparison can be instituted between them, do we owe the most; from which may we expect in the future the greatest benefits? So far scientific inquiry is in the saddle and leads the field. Yet is it not evident that for some reason, since our attention has been mainly directed to the external world and material things and our knowledge of them so marvelously increased, the human spirit has suffered hardship and become of less account, human life diminished in importance, and our hearts depressed? Can it be truly said that during the reign of science, during the centuries of its triumphant progress, we have attained a higher standard of humanity, justice, honor, or chivalry? Is there to be found around us today an increase of happiness, any clear or certain evidence of higher and more hopeful spirits? Has brute force disappeared, or given way in any degree to reasonableness or courtesy? Can we assert that truth, beauty, and nobility are held in greater respect than in earlier days, or that in our needs and requirements there has been any spiritual progress? If science, then, has not carried the banner of progress to the heights we hoped to climb, the causes of our discontent are not far to seek. We asked her to perform an impossible task to which she never addressed herself, and with which she was not concerned. In her own and chosen undertaking, the study of nature and of our material surroundings, the successes of science have surpassed all expectation. The failure was not hers but ours. It was a cardinal error to assume that she could make any substantial contribution to the improvement of human nature, or to the elevation and refinement of human character or human conduct. Intoxicated by the conquests of physical nature, we supposed them sufficient for all our needs, and in our exultation forgot the simple truth that man is not merely a reasoning being, that knowledge of nature's ways do not satisfy his heart, nor does a purely intellectual diet feed his moral and spiritual being, his ideals, aims, and aspirations.

You recall Pope's famous line, "The proper study of mankind is man." And we may, I think, at least agree that in the interests of any form of civilization yet devised the conquest of man over himself, over his will and passions, over his animal nature, is of no less importance than the subjugation and control of the forces of nature.

If any subject occupies the public mind today it is education. But what kind of education have we in view? To educate the mind is difficult enough, but how much more troublesome the education of the emotions. Accuracy of thinking is not, as is commonly supposed, a rarer thing than refinement or delicacy of sensibility. In my belief it is much more widely distributed and more highly appreciated. Far more care is given by the state to the education of the intellect than of the feelings. The values of quick wits, a good memory, sharp intelligence, and exact thinking are universally recognized. But where are we to look for a similar recognition of the values of right feeling, of taste, of delicate discernment, of quality rather than force of mind, of sensitivity and sympathy in social intercourse, which are powers and faculties of the soul? By his taste we distinguish the scholar from the pedant, by his possession of taste, the gentleman from the barbarian. It is the standard of refinement prevailing among its citizens that exalts a nation, and by which a civilization may be judged. Brains and knowledge you may have in abundance and yet remain a savage. Examples are not far to seek in the world today. Look around and you will, I think, become vividly aware that to educate and discipline the soul is of no less vital consequence in any society than to accumulate information or add a cubit to its intellectual stature.

Suppose we were to give our thoughts another turn. "After all," remarked a Cambridge mathematician of *Paradise Lost*, "what does it prove?" And clearly, if exact knowledge or power over nature's forces be your aim, poetry, music, and the other arts will not hasten to your aid. If you are asked of the frieze of the Parthenon, or a melody of Handel's, or one of Turner's landscapes, "What does it prove?" you have to confess that it proves nothing. Not one of these or similar works demonstrates any proposition or leads to any conclusion of which you can make any obvious or profitable use. The fine arts labor under this awkward disability. They have little connection with the multitudinous activities or undertakings of the community. Yet if the pursuit of the arts does nothing more than to bring or confer happiness upon the human family, we cannot go far wrong in their company, for in the word "happiness" is summed up all the desires, all the needs of mankind, yes, even of angels, or the gods themselves.

That brilliant Irishman, Richard Steele, lost an estate by his choice of a party. But he preferred, he said, the state of his mind to the state of his fortune. The fine arts prove nothing. To speak of them in connection with our social problems seems utterly irrelevant. Statesmen pay small attention to them. One hears no mention of them at elections. Politely accepted they may be, and allowed to be ornamental, nonetheless also tacitly assumed to be of small consequence. The urgent question arises whether a man's state of mind or a people's state of mind is in fact of minor or trifling importance, or on the contrary, as Steele perceived, of major and transcendent importance. What can be more useful than a state of mind? It is the most useful of all things, an end in itself. For a happy state of mind is a heavenly state of mind, and takes you back to the Garden of Eden before the Fall, before the desire for knowledge brought about the great catastrophe.

To claim the poets, painters, musicians as the best friends and allies of civilization may very well be regarded by the majority of men as a mere extravagance, a high and mighty claim, not to be seriously entertained. The answer is, a still more exalted claim has been advanced for them. Let me recall to you the attitude of that remarkable genius, painter, poet, citizen of London, William Blake, toward the fine arts. Blake went much further than his eighteenth-century predecessors in respect for their efficacy as missionaries of civilization. He advanced a singular doctrine. They were, he held, the truest interpreters and representatives of Christianity itself. Nor was this opinion set forth by Blake in any vague or nebulous fashion, but with the most intense conviction of its truth, in the most distinct, forthright, and astonishing language. He identified Christianity with the love and practice of the fine arts. Not only did he assert categorically that Christianity is art and art Christianity; not only did he say "Jesus and the Apostles were all artists," that "Prayer is the study of art, Praise is the practice of art"; not only did he proclaim that the three sons of Noah, who survived the Flood, were to be symbolically understood as Poetry, Painting, and Music: he went so far as to make the somewhat alarming declaration, "A poet, a painter, a musician, an architect, the man or woman who is not one of these is not a Christian." When you have taken breath and pondered these remarks, you may conclude them symptoms of evident lunacy, nothing more than the excursions of an unbalanced mind, a mere froth of wild words. It would be, I think, much too rash and hasty a judgment. The world at large is not interested in ordinary men who go the way it goes, however successfully. It is interested in men who go their own way, artists, poets, dreamers, who are without common sense, but have some kind of uncommon sense, which startles and kindles the mind of the observer, men who stumble and fall when they walk, but at moments attain the miracle of flight. "There is something in the madness of this man," said Wordsworth of William Blake, "which interests me more than the sanity of Lord Byron and Walter Scott." "This man," wrote Swinburne, "had never lived in the low places of thought." Verdicts like these give us pause.

What, then, was Blake's meaning and contention? His doctrine, however extravagantly expressed, is easily comprehended. The fine arts are essentially religious, and for this reason: they interpret the world and human life in the language of the soul, as distinguished from reason and science, which attempt to interpret them exclusively in terms of the intellect. To the assumption that reason is the only avenue to truth Blake opposed an inflexible and unyielding front, as did Pascal when he wrote, "The heart has its reasons of which reason knows nothing." Blake believed with passionate conviction that man's reason, enslaved in the service of his bodily necessities, is lost and cannot but be lost when it attempts to enter the realm of supersensuous reality, the region of ultimate and innermost truth, when it presumptuously proposes to unveil the last secrets of the universe. It is lost as hopelessly as the geologist or mathematician is lost in the inner and spiritual realms. What has physics or chemistry to say of our ideals and sympathies, our hopes and fears and longings? Are there no such things; are these words without meaning?

When you rule out all evidence save the evidence of material things, supplied by the five bodily senses, "The universe belies you and your heart refutes a hundred times the mind's conceit." In this matter Blake was disturbed by no doubts, no hesitations. As when, for example, he said of Flaxman's death, "I cannot think of death as more than the going out of one room into another." Refusing to accept a mechanical universe, mere physical phenomena, as the final truth, the reality of all realities, he held a very different creed. Poetry, painting, music disclosed, as religion also discovered, a depth and mystery in the world beyond all physical investigation, and were in consequence at one with Christianity upon the great and paramount issues. They should be regarded as windows into the transcendental world, invisible to mortal sight, presenting wider prospects, a vision of beauty in closest correspondence with the aspirations and affections of mankind. They were, in William Blake's own charming phrase, "three powers in man of conversing with Paradise."

Such then, in briefest outline, is Blake's doctrine. Can it be accepted? It assigns to the aspirations and intimations of our innermost being a higher authority than the authority of the intellect. They penetrate, it asserts, more deeply into the true heart of the universe than the logical understanding, they bring with them "authentic tidings of invisible things." This philosophy runs counter—let us be clear on the matter—to the strongest tides of modern thought. The world, however, is not yet at an end, and there are centuries yet to come. We must expect as many and amazing alterations of thought in the future as the past has ever seen.

We approach now the main issue. To the arts has been assigned an exalted rank above all other undertakings, a peculiar respect, reverence, authority. They appear to have their natural home in a region impenetrable by reason. They point to a world above our heads, a transcendental world, in which, if anywhere, we may hope to find the fulfillment of our heart's desire. Does such a world exist, or is it a mirage, a lying vision only? Here is the great divide, the momentous parting of the ways in human thought. Here every man must make his choice. Here on one side stand the rationalists, men who decline, like St. Thomas, to advance beyond the evidence of the senses, to believe until they have seen with their eyes, touched, and handled, the men who put their trust in the human intellect, its findings and no other. And here in opposition are the men of religion, the poets and artists who place their trust in the inner vision, the intimations of the soul and its affections.

And not only the men of religion and the poets. Listen to Nietzsche, that hard, disillusioned thinker. "There is in all great art an enigmatic profundity, an infinity of background." And again: "The man of philosophic turn has a foreboding that beneath this reality in which we live and move and have our being another and altogether different reality lies concealed." Yes, they have a foreboding not easily exorcised. Keep company with the arts and it will continue to haunt you. They have apparently nothing more than a decorative value, and nonetheless possess a supreme value. They appear to be concerned with matters of no great consequence, and yet, it seems, introduce you to matters of vital consequence. Keep company with them, and without warning, reading a poem, listening to a piece of music, looking at a picture, you may be entangled, as Nietzsche says, in the infinities. One never knows when the heavens may open, and in the shock of this bewilderment, face to face with the immeasurable universe, a man looks about him with new awareness, new apprehension. It is then that suddenly the whole scene of existence is perceived in its overwhelming immensity, its true dimensions. What may it or may it not contain? It is then that the values of the fleeting world are weighed in the balance. Even the plain man is exposed to this strange peril. He finds an inexplicable fascination in these enigmatic arts. He may not take them seriously. Yet some secret sympathy, some inborn loyalty draws him, do what he will, to admire, to listen, and to gaze. So at any moment he may be swept away into the deep sea and cannot but inquire, "What means all this?"

When you enter the temple of the arts you enter a building dedicated to the Muses, and the soul is there disturbed by a sense of how great and terrible, how strange and beautiful is this universe of ours. Make human life as trivial as you please, there remains the simple, positive, undeniable fact, among the other facts—the eating and drinking, walking and talking—that we are taking part in cosmic affairs, of a magnitude beyond all imagination to compass or language to express. All finite things have their roots in the infinite, and if you wish to understand life at all, you cannot tear it out of its context. And that context, astounding even to bodily eyes, is the heaven of stars and the incredible procession of the great galaxies.

In poetry, like its sister arts, you discern—it is common knowledge—not only a peculiar aloofness from life's daily routine, but a singular language. By this idiom the arts are known, the form and grace, the celestial quality, the rhythm of their speech. And what is rhythm, and why celestial? Celestial since, however it be defined, it is, in fact, the speech of nature and of life. Unseen and unobserved it rules the movements of the heavens, guides the atom and the star, swings the seasons and the days and nights. It illuminates the world in the passage of light, controls the winds and waves, all the organic processes of our bodies, the sleeping and waking, the pulsing of the heart and lungs. The laws of rhythm are the laws that guide the whole fabric of creation, a structure harmonious in all its manifestations, the smallest as the greatest. To this voice from the depths, this music of the spheres, the soul, the organ of feeling, as distinguished from the understanding, is attuned. There is, as Aristotle's pregnant sentence expresses it, "a kind of relationship between the soul and harmonies and rhythms." All art is tuneful—not music only. A painting, a statue, a building, each in its own manner, is a melodious creation. Have you observed that a tune has a secret virtue, unique and all its own? It is a work of magic. It possesses occult properties. When a tune falls on your ear you respond with instant sympathy. You accept without question the suggested measure, you surrender with what Schopenhauer described as "blind consent" to its enchantment, its peculiar spell. You cannot deny, argue with, or contradict a tune. You cannot take another point of view or advance a contrary proposition. The tune is your master, you its spellbound servant. And in the arts this peculiar language is everywhere and by all men understood. It is the soul's native tongue, and needs no learning.

There is such a thing as an art of life. Civilization may be described as itself a work of art. As in a Gothic minster you have a great building, the work not of one but many minds and hands, so civilization is a work of communal art, which includes and is indebted to them all. It is a piece of racial architecture, a realization, in its law and order, its etiquette of customs and behavior, its institutions and ceremonials, of a people's tastes and preferences. It may with truth be regarded as an application to political and civic life, to social intercourse, of the distinction and beauty that delight us in music and poetry. For if beautiful behavior be not good behavior, it is something very like it. "In a thoroughly humanized society," wrote Santayana, "everything—clothes, speech, manners, government—is a work of art." One might, indeed, call its civilization the speaking image of the entire community. In such a society every citizen is himself an artist, and has his share of responsibility as one of its architects.

So far from agreeing with Hegel that "thought and reflection have taken their flight above fine art," we must submit that, philosopher though he was, he had not attained so much as a glimmering recognition of its true character, or of its transcendent importance in human life. For art is not merely irreplaceable by any other agency. We can with confidence declare that to the arts, which may well be called divine, belongs a glorious privilege. They have made of beauty a guiding star. They have led mankind on the greatest of all its undertakings and supported it through all the wintry seasons of history. To them we owe the great unwritten principles, the immortal laws that have shaped and guided the conscience of the race. Had Blake been asked, "Should we be any worse off if these arts were to take wings and forsake this planet altogether?" he would have answered, "Deny humanity their guidance, and you stab it to the heart. You deprive it of all the spiritual interests, you drive it back into the aboriginal abyss, a naked animal, bereft of all its hard-won ethical conceptions, as of justice and equity, of honor and humanity, of law and magnanimity and duty." How right was Tolstoy when he said: "Art is a great matter, and its task is enormous."

No one will deny that modern societies, the whole world over, are dominated by cupidity, by greed for possession, for wealth and power. And, as far as I can see, there is no sure shield against the tyranny of this ruinous passion for possession save a transference of our affections, if this be possible, from possession to admiration, from immoderate craving for wealth and power to an intense longing for beauty and excellence. Must we forever continue to think in terms of profit and loss, of all life's lower and lesser interests? As the Greeks knew, "The beautiful is hard, hard to judge, hard to win, hard to keep." Yet the love of beauty exists, an ineradicable passion in every human heart, together with a marvelous capacity for its appreciation. Whatever else be given us, without beauty we can never be at peace or at rest. In all forms of beauty, mankind will never cease to take delight till the world ends. Nor can better testimony to the significance and worth of the gentle and healing arts be offered than this, that the works the great masters never grow old. How reluctant is mankind to part from them!

The centuries pass, the generations come and go, but in each there springs up once more a passion for the past and all its lovely creations. Though we are gone, Persephone will still gather her flowers in Sicilian Enna, Faust will brood eternally among his books, Hamlet will never cease to ponder the mysteries on the battlements of Elsinore.

A New View of the World

GORDON KEITH CHALMERS

War brings many men and women to their finest hour. This war is able to do because it is a purge and a reduction agent. In wartime neuroses disappear, people return to plain talk about discipline; half the nonsense of popular psychology, self-pity, even greed and sloth are burnt out of men. Katharine Cornell has revived the Chekhov play, *The Sisters*, written about 1900. Its theme is boredom in the provinces—oh, we'll never get to Moscow. How silly it sounds in wartime, how simple to our ears are the selfish problems of mean, little, indulgent people. Let them, we say, get up and out of themselves and do one generous free deed.

War also is a reduction agent, simplifying all desires to one desire, all duties to one duty. No fighting man finds his resolution "sicklied o'er with the pale cast of thought." He acts before thinking, the one necessary thought having been given by the war itself. That thought, of course, is *victory*. Thus out of warfare come some of our most thrilling certainties: "Praise the Lord and pass the ammunition," with its seventeenth-century counterpart, "Fear God and keep your powder dry"; "Don't fire 'til you see the whites of their eyes"; "Oh, Passerby, tell the Lacedaemonians that we lie here fulfilling their commands."

The study for war may omit altogether an inquiry into ends. During war everyone knows the end, and, to play with the metaphor, he knows the sides, too—the enemy's side and our side. For loyalty, sacrifice, love of country and hearth we rely largely on what has been taught before war began. The whole study for war itself, once war begins, is a study of process—how to wage it. This study accounts now for most university and college teaching—mathematics for the sake of navigation, submarine detection, ballistics, weather forecasting; languages for the sake of liaison work or Army and Navy intelligence; history for the sake of indoctrination and the exposition of war aims. Education for war is education in processes, and it is properly called technical training.

But though war brings many men and women to their finest hour it brings beyond question to mankind and to most of its wretched victims the worst moments, hours, and decades imaginable in all history. The truly finest hours of men have been peaceful. These may be distinguished from the fine hours of warfare by the fact that in peace man's fineness is more complex than in war. While in war a hero may ignore ends and devote his whole mind to process (being certain of the one, all embracing, simple end, victory), in peace no heroic deed is done without an elaborate and vivid awareness of ends. Who are the enemies in peace? They are subtle, hidden, sly serpents, wolves in sheep's clothing. To know them, to know the fine shade of right which marks it from the similar shade of wrong, to know when pride turns virtue into vice, when sacrifice becomes vainglory, when ideals become hypocrisy—this knowledge requires the most manly skill and courage available to men. To study for war is to study processes; to study for peace is to study ends, values, purposes, virtues, ideas. Perhaps education in the past twenty-five years was not really education for peace. In any case, it failed to help keep the world peaceful.

During the past quarter century we have said much about finding a moral equivalent for war. We have tried to devise a cause, a grand world cause of peace, in the hope that men would commit themselves to it with the abandon and fervor characteristic of soldiers in combat. The cause has been elaborated into protocols, courts, committees, and conferences, but as it affects the individual man it is abstract, enormous, and unreal. Its validity does not compare with moral realities of the fighting man—*dulce et decorum est pro patria mori.*

The effort to find a moral equivalent for war merits reflection in 1943 when war is showing Americans in Africa and Australia moral forces in themselves of which they had never dreamed. In the twenties and thirties when liberalism tried and failed—tried at Versailles, Geneva, The Hague, Washington, Paris, Weimar, London, and Berlin—what was happening to education? What did in fact occur in the schools and universities in those years was the effect of intellectual forces much prior in our history to 1914-1918, but it is sufficient for our purpose to examine education in the interbellum years, when, it happens, the Occident told itself so generally that it must find a moral equivalent for war. The clearest tell-tale of popular and university education is literature and scholarship. The period under view was the period of the Left Bank, of F. Scott Fitzgerald, Eugene O'Neill, James Joyce, and Henry Mencken. The novelists and playwrights of the time did not think themselves particularly wicked; with Nietzsche they fancied themselves "beyond good and evil." Scholarship also indulged in genial amorality. Ideas and value judgments counted less to the learned than philology and grammar. Historians thought less and less about the choices men have made and more and more about the circumstances which surrounded their decisions. Anatole France said that the critic is he who records the adventures of his soul among masterpieces; his followers doubted if there are masterpieces at all, since they held, quoting another age of relativism, de gustibus non est disputandum. The psychologists laughed the will out of their textbooks, and schools were founded on the idea that a child may grow up by dealing wholly with desire and satisfaction. Pavlov's dogs eclipsed the Decalogue; conditioning became the word for education, and all scholars, envious of the measurements and observations of biology and physics, fell to recording conditions. The lust for description without judgment was so deep that classicists, historians, sociologists, economists, political scientists, modern and oriental linguists outshouted each other in their claims that never were their pages soiled with reference to value. The illusion spread that all value is subjective; only the physicist is objective, but the others may hope for a kind of minor salvation by renouncing so far as possible what critical powers God gave them.

Morality had been transferred from the individual to the group—a notion resurrected from Rousseau, the deity of the New Education, who said that man is naturally good, convention only makes him wicked; so the real wickedness lies wholly in bad conventions. Conventions being "conditions," the hounds of learning bayed after conditions wherever the scent blew.

This is how we thought. It is how we think now in school, in college, in church, on the stage, in the publishing houses, in the editorial rooms of the critical journals. There are bright exceptions, but if one wants to characterize the higher learning and the higher teaching and the higher thesis-writing in America, here is the body of the matter. The proposition has been put time and again by the social scientists and educationists in their insistence upon the omnific importance of conditions; for the scholars it was put explicitly and by implication by philologians, who said that the young men should devote their time in college to the words and grammar; there will be time enough afterwards to think of what the words say. The matter was stated for literary men by Lewis Mumford and numerous others in their retractions, as the war approached, culminating in the bitter essay on writers of his own generation by Archibald MacLeish and called *The Irresponsibles*.

The proposition was put by numerous students of these scholars and writers, one of the best-written and most effective statements of it being the book by a young graduate of Smith College called *The Wave of the Future*. If you remember this dangerous little essay you will reflect that it stated the accepted educational doctrine of the time, namely that learning is adjustment. Hitler and Mussolini, said the author, have seen the wave of the future and have leapt upon it; the wise man will adjust himself to the wave.

The chief mark of the period when men sought a moral equivalent for war is the learned and thoughtful effort to abandon morality, to pretend that it is unimportant or does not exist, that there are no standards, indeed, no criticism (remembering that Κριτής means judge), no power of judgment within a man who, like Pavlov's dogs, is fit subject for conditioning. This is what we studied, preached, and taught.

But the moral equivalent for war must first of all be moral. It must in addition be something available to a man in his privacy, his pride, his love. To figure in the thoughts of a brave and sensitive man it must lead him to certainties comparable to the certainties with which the fighting man begins, comparable to the sureness with which men embark on any circumscribed but bold adventure, such as the physical adventure of battle or the sea. I have referred to the near-certainties of hazardous action. Here is another: "Shipwrecked mariners perished on this coast bid you set sail; many a ship when we were lost, weathered the gale."

To the man of action there are certainties or near-certainties of what the ends are, certainties or near-certainties of who and what are the enemy. To the man of free action there are near-certainties concerning the enemy within ourselves, and certainties of whom and what we may trust as our own hearts' ally.

The intellectual and educational forces at work in America at the moment are not, in my opinion, pointed toward leading men to anything like this state of mind when the war is over. There are instead, two great and numerously supported movements in education: one, proposing to improve the rudiments of technical training (largely arithmetic), and another, concerned with informing people about social and international plans. In a small way, both of these are all right, but let us examine them.

American education has changed over from peace to war by becoming technical. Thank heaven for this. The education of Germany and Japan became technical over a decade ago, and without all-out technical training we cannot defeat our enemies. But when victory is won in the field, what then? Already answers are being given, outlining how to reconvert American schools and colleges to peace. Those responsible for the Army and Navy training programs in the colleges have said sometimes privately, sometimes in public, that the national training schemes will probably provide a means whereby schools backward in mathematics will be led or coerced into doing a real job with arithmetic. This might be a good thing. The men now responsible for technical training for war know what *hard* subjects are, and, happily, they favor them above easy subjects. Discipline of a sort will be revived in schools. In a small way this also is a good thing. Some of these officers and civilians go on to say that there should be cultural education, "culture" being necessary to any enduring pursuit of elaborate technical study. This also may be a good thing. It may be, but I doubt it, because "culture," "cultural background," "tradition" for its own sake, "a little sense of heritage," may be very bad things. They may be bad in the same fashion that a little religion or a little art or a little learning is a dangerous thing. The danger arises when these elements of life involving value are a decoration to life rather than its architect; the danger arises because peace, like war, has been conceived by the nineteenth and twentieth centuries as primarily a matter of process. Any educational system concerned first with process is bound, human failure being what it is, to be mistaken about ends.

Another group of planners for postwar education imagine that the conversion of schools to peace is as easy as beating swords into plowshares. "For the techniques of war," they say, "substitute the techniques of peace." The techniques of peace are thought to be social techniques—international plans for collective security and domestic plans for distribution and social security. These also are good things. But they are not matters of the very first importance for schools and colleges. Yet the peace-plan pamphlets and books almost invariably refer to these problems as the curriculum of education for peace. Here, for example, is the proposal of an official committee reporting to the American Youth Commission, saying that the following subjects should be studied and debated by high school pupils: "housing, conservation of natural and human resources, community planning, cooperatives, pressure groups and their methods of influencing legislation, the stock exchange, corporations, labor organizations, the industries of the nation, various forms of municipal government, governmental services such as those of the Departments of Agriculture, Commerce, and Labor, the origin and nature of money and systems of exchange, international relations, consumers' needs and investments." Peace planners suggest similar studies of the American electoral system and economic problems and economic geography. All this for schoolboys! Yes, perhaps. If there is time. Certainly study clubs, editors, schoolteachers, ministers, and other community leaders should read such technical information. School children only if they have time. Only if, after learning the early disciplines which will help instruct the soul, help reveal man as he is, help mature them, there remains time.

The fault of such proposals is not only that they imply that such studies are of first importance and sufficient; the fault lies also, sad to say, in their success. Last summer, for example, the writers of historical textbooks for the schools complained that they could not sell them unless they inserted new title-pages calling them social studies. History is a way to think; so is literature. So much talk about social problems has displaced the very elementary studies which, when mastered, make these elaborate and complex problems intelligible. Schoolboys have been deprived of the opportunity to learn the nature of individual good and bad on the pretense that a few slogans concerning the good and bad for the group may be substituted.

To improve the rudiments of technical education and to instruct the young about peace plans can hardly be called evil. The danger in these two movements lies in the probability that being of some worth they will delude us into thinking they really bear upon the terrific educational problem which confronts us. If these two slight reforms provide the dogma of postwar education, they may prove disastrous. By disastrous I mean that they may breed the next war; for both of these types of study are technical, not critical; both lead the young mind to dwell upon and master processes; both consume the precious time allotted to a youth to inform himself about himself; that is, about human nature, about the ends of manhood, and thus debar him from his best heritage as a human being. Chancellor Brüning, describing the rise of totalitarianism in Europe, said that if he should assign the catastrophe to any one cause it would be the passionate confidence of the postwar European universities in technology.

What is needed, educationally, is not an improved technique nor a new technique, but a new view of the world. By this I do not mean a new charter for the world, important as that is politically. What we need educationally applies to the way people privately think and make up their minds. Politically, we surely need a new order, and to a degree popular education will have to propagandize for this, to a great degree editors, luncheon clubs, ministers, foreign affairs councils, professors, and teachers should study, discuss, write, and re-write peace plans. But in the hearts and minds of school children and college students what is needed most is a way to look, an understanding which is, philosophically speaking, so new to our century that new teachers must be trained to teach it, old teachers led in their own hearts to a transvaluation of values.

The requirements of this new view become evident if we reflect on what is implied by our peace plans. The peace plans call for imperial responsibility without the abuses of empire, and they trust us, trust the American public, to refrain from abuses. For a protracted period following the most expensive of all wars we propose to police a large part of the world. How sorely we shall be tempted to make the vanquished and the backward peoples pay for our beneficent administration! How easy it will be to cloak our lust for an American Century with fine phrases equivalent to Manifest Destiny and the White Man's Burden, backing up our hypocrisy with facts and figures about high taxes at home and the necessity to placate American Industry and Labor with preferential tariffs, colonial privileges, and other means of paying for a two-ocean navy! No nation in all the world can contribute to peace and get rich. It is easier for a camel to go through the eye of a needle. America, the land of gigantic exploitation, must adopt voluntary near-poverty. This means that Congress must show self-restraint. It means the voters must do so, it means the public must instinctively sense the fallacies in journalistic big talk whether uttered by editors, politicians, movie magnates, or anybody.

In addition to withholding our own hand, we must help govern parts of the world and set an example of government, and we must very likely play an important part in the Orient, a part similar to that heretofore played with unsatisfactory effect by our intelligent and highly educated ally, Britain.

For the sake of bringing law and justice to distant parts of the world British education in the past century devoted itself to discipline, in part to a stupid and naïve kind of discipline, but in part to a real discipline of the mind. Americans cannot hope to be of use in the government of the world without discipline in education, discipline not simply as good as the British discipline but better.

Thus for Americans there are three obvious requirements of the peace: self-restraint, discipline, and a knowledge of the East. Self-restraint and discipline sound like negative virtues, but no lively and durable notion of them proves, on extensive thought, to be merely negative. A man and a nation of men will withhold their hands only if they know something better for themselves than what they might have stolen. The something better requires faith, imagination, humor, wit, detachment, and a kind of large confident freedom. While as a nation we are not famous for self-restraint, these positive concomitants of it are not alien to us. The New View of the World must be built upon them.

We are here to talk about postwar education, and we may have hoped to avoid a discussion of religion. But I doubt if we can. We may have hoped to avoid a discussion of ethics, but ethics proves to be the center of the problem. We might prefer to devote our time to discussing the rationale of peace—our relations with the Orient and Latin America and the improvement of social conditions in the United States. Much, surely, must be done with the rationale of peace, but the ethical and religious parts of the problem are so gigantic and their solution is so clearly our obligation as teachers, I must omit talk about the rationale of peace.

Again religion and peace would fill a large book; without it, little may be said of ethics and peace. For example, the recent reiteration by André Maurois of the old truth that knowledge must follow belief, never precede it, calls in question most university learning as we have known it. To put some limits on this paper, however, I shall pass by this profound puzzlement of our lives with the flat opinion that the sterility of university learning will increase if its ignorance of religion increases.

Ethics falls in the middle of our problem, and to ethics I

shall devote what time remains. I have used the words morals and ethics so frequently and with such wide implications that many may wonder what I mean. By them I mean what man really is and really does, I mean the study required by the ancient command, "Know Thyself." Thus, much of extreme puritanism would prove not moral but immoral for precisely the same reason that much that was extreme in the period of the Restoration was immoral—both were inaccurate. Each rendered an account of man which by no means conforms with Everyman as we know him, as we know him with precision and vividness in all those sharp and clear revelations he has left of himself, first of all in our own hearts and the sorrows, joys, failures, or heroism of our intimates, second in those hours of self-revelation recorded by the most trustworthy and precise recorders of human thought and action, the poets, philosophers, biographers, chroniclers, historians, letter-writers, saints, heroes, and intelligent rascals whose words and thoughts have been written down.

The chief business of postwar education will be to teach young people to know human nature as it is, to be accurate about it, and to think of it with imagination, warmth, and courage.

Accuracy begins with the letter and the number, but it hardly stops there. The eyes and ears are poor witnesses, said Heraclitus, if the heart is barbarous. Beyond the accuracy of the word is the higher accuracy, the accuracy of the meaning. It is inaccurate, for example, to say that Robert Frost is a New England poet, or a nature poet; when Jowett translates the funeral oration of Pericles as if Athens had been a liberal nineteenth-century democracy, the thinking has been inaccurate. What is meant by "charity" in the thirteenth chapter of Corinthians? To translate the word as "love" and confuse it with romantic love, reading the chapter in this sense in the marriage service is inaccurate. Such problems, thousands of them, make up the large problem of deciding wisely about ourselves.

The outstanding educational reform of the past twenty years has endeavored to achieve one important end, to recall higher education to primary concern for human values. I refer, of course, to the effort of Mr. Hutchins and his associates at Chicago and St. John's College. They say that the chief concern of intelligent men is what man hath made of man. Their polemics in behalf of this ancient truth have been elaborate and logical, their syllogisms often flawless, their reasoning often irrefutable. Sad to say, however, the spirit of argument has entered very far into their thinking itself, and their insistence upon the trivium and quadrivium falls victim to the arid dangers of the scholasticism whence these disciplines come. Their account of learning suggests that dialectic characterizes the thinking mind; in their hands the subtle and precise affirmations of mankind appear to be primarily a series of necessary steps in argument; theirs is the neo-classical spirit. In fact, the great books of the world involve much more than dialectic. The ancients called this extra something rhetoric, but even that discipline, bound as it is to its origins in the arts of persuasion and oratory, hardly describes the extra something I speak of.

That extra involves the intuition, the sensitive perception of nuances, the imagination. Dialectics is involved in the study I speak of: the study itself is literature—literature, be it understood, comprising not only poems and plays, but laws, prayers, and all the most meaningful utterances of men. How readily the study of man's account of himself falls down from the high level where the search is for an accurate account of human nature to polemic and dialectic, where the ulterior motive is reform! Hesketh Pearson, the biographer of Bernard Shaw, exemplifies this phenomenon in the lives of men of genius with Shaw himself, who as he aged tried less and less to hold a mirror up to nature and followed more and more the easier course of preaching.

The principal study for peace is literature. But to many scholars and critics, literature itself is most interesting because of its techniques. To them it is like the talk of the talkative wife whose husband was up for desertion.

"Why did you leave her?" asked the judge.

"She talks and talks. She talks morning, noon, and night."

"Well, what does she talk about?"

"She don't say."

The most important thing about literature is what it says.

The study of literature as we have known it is bound up largely with the past. So charming and so pure and so adventuresome does life appear in retrospect that we think of it and sometimes re-enact it or rebuild its houses, courts, and cathedrals, with nostalgia. Miniver Cheevy in Robinson's poem was such a romantic:

> Miniver sighed for what was not,
>   And dreamed, and rested from his labors;
> He dreamed of Thebes and Camelot,
>   And Priam's neighbors.
>   * * *
> Miniver loved the Medici,
>   Albeit he had never seen one;
> He would have sinned incessantly
>   Could he have been one.
>   * * *
> Miniver Cheevy, born too late,
>   Scratched his head and kept on thinking;
> Miniver coughed, and called it fate,
>   And kept on drinking.

There is at least a fraction of truth in Carl Sandburg's line, "I tell you the past is a bucket of ashes." Evidently Henry Ford knows little history, but he voiced a valid emotion when he said to the undergraduate who had taken him from the Morris works at Cowley to the cloisters and walls of Oxford, "Take me back to the twentieth century." Why, for example, should it be that at the mention of a classicist we think first of all of a man concerned with the past? Why should we not think first of a man especially competent to deal with our first-class evidence concerning human nature? Too many scholars have taken pride in the mere antiquity of their subject.

Let us face the embarrassing fact. The scholars and teachers responsible for making available to the life of the twentieth century the wisdom of ancient times have largely failed. Perhaps they have spoiled its usefulness to us by conveying the illusion that the past is important because it happened long ago, forgetting that the only subject of first importance is human experience. All of us, I think, are convinced that the fault lies not with the quality of ancient wisdom but with the whole educational effort, in its social, moral, and religious setting. The past has much to tell us as we try to instruct ourselves for peace. Perhaps the circumstances of 1943 are such that little or none of it can be brought to us in the old way. Perhaps schoolboys never again will be able to start their quest for the bright light of Socrates and the strong knowledge of Euripides by parsing sentences from Xenophon's *Anabasis*. But somehow man's intuitive perceptions about himself and his sense of salvation and nemesis must, if humanly possible, be conveyed to the young of the 1940's and 1950's.

The knowledge I speak of is not common in the history of any one nation; the past three thousand years the world around contained more of it than any one country, more than any man's lifetime, ours included. Perhaps in spite of our failure to make use of what lies at hand from ancient Egypt, Greece, Palestine, Rome, and Europe we may, with the new orientation of our political life, be able to study along with those familiar to scholarship a new set of classics, the classics of the East, and perhaps we may succeed in studying them as contemporaries, not as charming antiques.

Professor John Erskine and the other despoilers of the ancients pretend to make them contemporary by reducing heroes to the stature of little men. This, of course, is journalistic nonsense. Hollywood stuff. Any utterance of distinction—that is, any deed or statement of absolutely first class—may appear contemporary only to the man of imagination. Imagination rightly understood, affords the key to the New View of the World. That the imagination may be schooled, enriched, and enlarged has been proved by all the truly great teachers.

When modern education ceased to be literary it gradually ceased to school the imagination. Your modern man of intellect like as not will have mature reasoning powers and the emotions of a child. The feelings have mistakenly been isolated from thinking, the sorry result being the slipshod practice which so often has paraded behind the banner of progressive education. To separate thinking and feeling has been as silly as to divorce theology and metaphysics, religion and learning. The schooled emotions at once instruct the intellect and are schooled by it. Only when they work in harmony, thought, and feeling so interrelated as to be inseparable, is any durable thinking done. You can name no humanistic work of the first order about which this is not true.

Literature has suffered at the hands of weak and sentimental votaries. Apologists for it still draw many of their polemics from the fanciful half-truths of Shelley's *Defense of Poetry*. Literature is called a tonic, a holiday, an escape; literature has been confined to the garden of belles lettres. Instead of understanding literature in the dimmest possible light, why not view it in the clear, endeavoring to grasp the dictum of Aristotle that the criterion of good poetry is its truth, that responsible fiction, fiction governed by universality, is truer than direct reporting.

Maxwell Anderson, examining his own plays and the musical comedies, tragi-comedies, and tragedies popular on Broadway, asked this question: "Why does the audience come to the theatre to look on while an imaginary hero is put to an imaginary trial and comes out of it with credit to the race and to himself?" He found the answer in the demand of the audience that the play prove "that men pass through suffering purified; that, animal though we are, despicable though we are in many ways, there is in us all some divine incalculable fire that urges us to be better than we are."

When modern education ceased to be literary, we gradually lost our understanding of the real nature and uses of imagination. We forgot that the disciplined imagination is ethical; we made it into a game of chasing butterflies. We forgot that the imagination leads on to reality and the truth. The change is revealed in a passage of the Behrman comedy, *The Pirate*, produced by the Lunts. Manuela says that to her "imagination is just an escape, the less it has to do with reality the better."

Serafin: "Well, you are the most extraordinary mixture of fantasy and realism it has ever been my good fortune to encounter."

Manuela: "Am I? Well, there is the practical world and the world of the imagination. I know which is which. I don't mix them."

Serafin: "There I don't agree with you. Not two separate worlds. One an extension of the other. If your imagination cannot give direction to reality—increase its potential—direct its course—then it is a mere lie, a mere delusion."

The importance of literature to common education is twofold: that it trains the imagination, and that it focuses the whole mind upon values, the apprehension of values being possible only to the disciplined imagination. A nation ignorant of literature is ethically ignorant. Once a student understands the innuendo, the overtone, the *double-entendre*, he begins naturally to sense all statements, not simply statements called literary, as expressions of value. Why are we troubled at Mr. Churchill's remark that Malta is as bright a diamond as shines in the King's crown? We like Mr. Churchill, and we think the phrase was a slip. But it worries us because we wonder if in spite of his statements in the Atlantic Charter Mr. Churchill still thinks too much about the jewels of an emperor.

We propose to the world a peace that is complex and mature, a peace in which we are determined that no empire, but the moral law shall be sovereign. Specifically, we propose that thousands of young Americans will go to Asia to live, many to Russia, to Europe and Africa, to collaborate with our allies and our former enemies in establishing and confirming peace. If what they do is to be both effective and intelligent, not only must they be educated and mature; the voters who support them must be familiar with human values. It is true that in addition to human knowledge, the leaders in the peace must be masters of elaborate technical knowledge—engineering, medicine, and law. One may expect a great expansion in graduate professional studies when the war is over. But all that skill, and all the accuracy of the planners will come to nothing unless founded upon a rich and lively sense of man, of man understood in the humanities, by a warm and imaginative familiarity with man known in stories, poems, prayers, laws, histories, and all those possessions of the heart and mind which distinguish us most clearly from beasts.

When the war is won, pure science will have its own struggles with the technical spirit, and in the modern world one could not hope for an intelligent and general apprehension of human nature unaccompanied by a bold and reflective and systematic inquiry into physical nature. In terms of general education, this implies a revival of school mathematics. I omit discussion of this only because the human studies are so much more likely to be ignored.

To train the imagination is to teach metaphors as well as syllogisms, and to recognize how man invents, how, to translate the ancient word ποιεῖν, the mind makes. Here is the mind in action, not passively learning. Here is the mind hazarding propositions to itself, propositions on which a man must live. Education along these lines involves commitments; commitments involve risks. Instead of saving himself from emotional involvement, the imaginative student gives his heart away, knowing well his peril if those ideas and people to whom he gives it prove treacherous.

Such a life has strictness and hazard, and holds before a man of daring and perception the brightest of all rewards. Such a life leads a man to near-certainties, not easily nor soon, but if he learns what he learns with his backbone as well as his head, it leads him surely.

> You will not find me changed from him you knew
> Only more sure of what I thought was true.

This promise of the young poet, Robert Frost, is the affirmation of a man of courage, imagination, and discernment. To live such a life one must learn with his whole being and live according to what he has learned. The life he will lead in consequence is a moral life, being confined to an accurate perception of man as we know him; such a life constitutes indeed, not only the moral substitute for combat, but the life itself for which crusaders in any age have been willing to undergo the indignities of war.

9970